I0763097

HAPP
CALM • PEACEFUL
PASSIVE • SAD
SERIOUS • PENSIVE
SENTIMENTAL • TOLERANT
DEPRESSED
30
29
28
27
26
25
24
23
22
21
20
19
18
17
SEMI-TRIAD
TRIADIC
HARMONY
SPLIT ANALOGOUS
COMPLE
TO USE
HILER CO

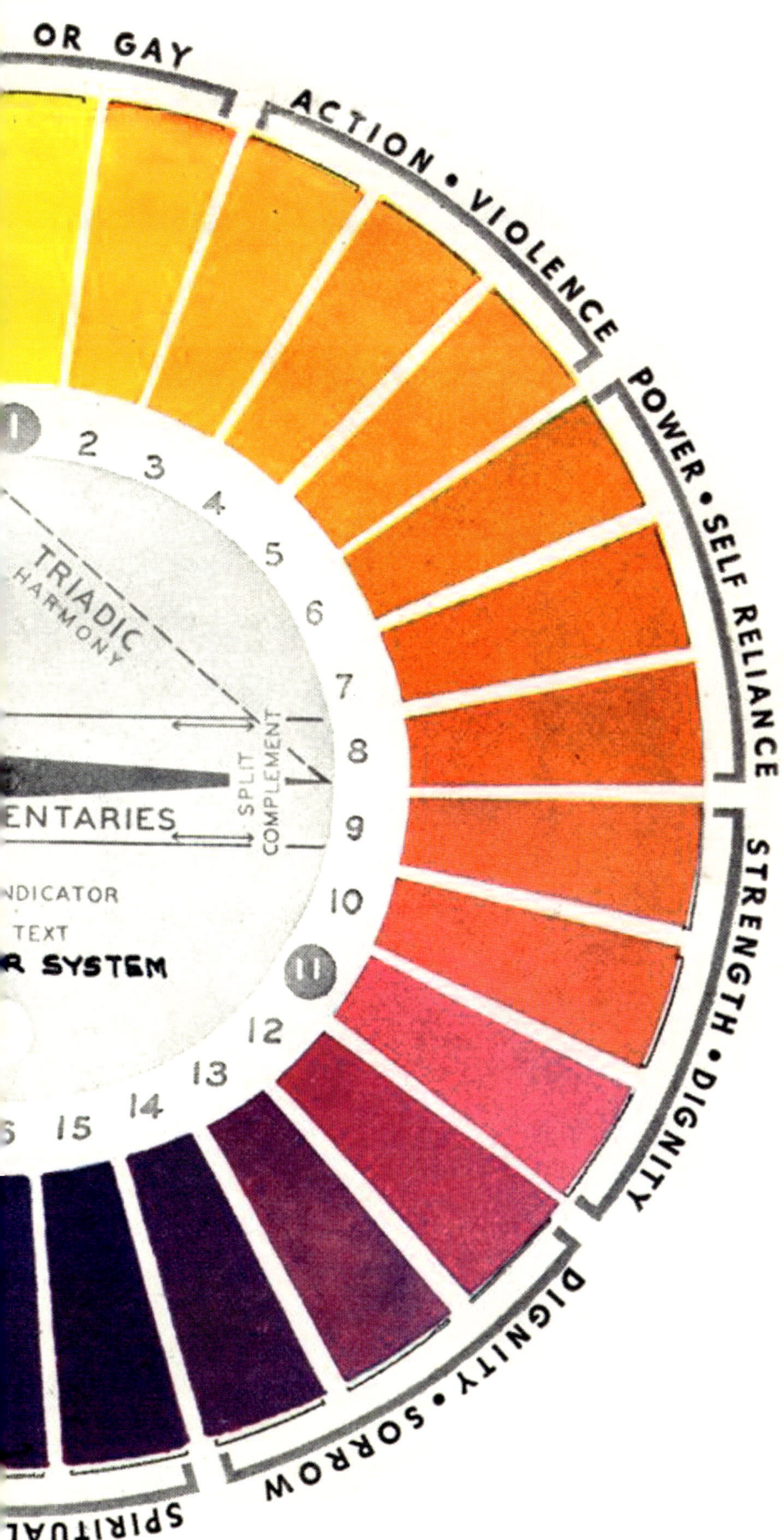
OR GAY
ACTION • VIOLENCE
POWER • SELF RELIANCE
STRENGTH • DIGNITY
DIGNITY • SORROW
SPIRITUAL
2
3
4
5
6
7
8
9
10
11
12
13
14
15
TRIADIC
HARMONY
SPLIT
COMPLEMENT
SPLIT
COMPLEMENT
ENTARIES
NDICATOR
TEXT
R SYSTEM

COCKTAILS
ESPRESSO

CARTE POSTALE

Correspondance

Adresse

je pars à la gare

CRAVAN

17 rue Jean de la Fontaine

75016 Paris

France

IL ÉTAIT UNE FOIS LA RKO
Hitchcock
NUMERO DEUX
TRAFIC
MES UNIVERSITES
Le sommeil paradoxal
ANDRÉ BAZIN
HISTOIRE DU CINÉMA
AMERICAN YOUTH
LOUIS JOUVET
ABEL GANCE
KITANO
ROSSELLINI
LE GOÛT DE LA BEAUTÉ
Pasolini et la mort

JEAN-LUC GODARD
ARTHUR CRAVAN
ŒUVRES
WARBURG
L'Atlas Mnémosyne
Aby Warburg
Arthur Cravan
Poète et Boxeur
la lime d'image
GODARD
GODARD
La Route de Silverado
COCTEAU
ET LE CINÉMA
DÉSORDRES
Philippe Azoury
Jean-Marc Lalanne
A HAWAIIAN READER
R.L.S.
MENSAGEM
CHESTERTON
ENFIN LE CINEMA!
WELLES

CRAVAN
PRÉ-ASSEMBLAGES
TRACE

POWER
ON
PHONES
SPEAKERS
ON
OFF
BASS
TREBLE
BALANCE
LEFT
LOUDNESS
OFF
ON
VOLUME
TAPE MONITOR
Sansui
AU-101
SOLID STATE STEREO AMPLIFIER

CRAVAN

COCKTAILS

Trocadéro

TABLE N° 20
COUVERTS .....

42%

TABLE N° 23
COUVERTS .....

53,50 g

63,09 g

17,93%

17,9%

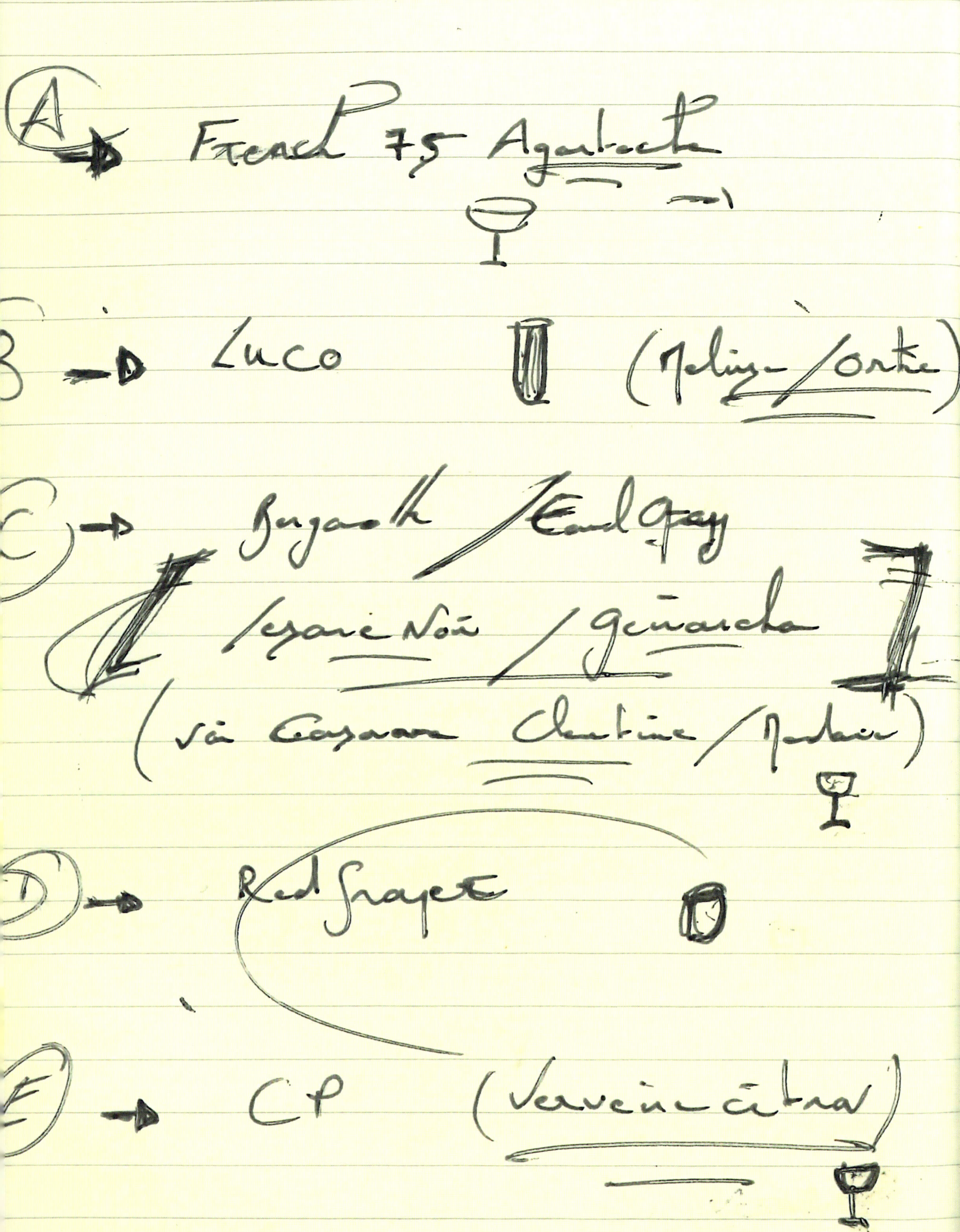
A
French 75
B
Luco
C
Bergamot / Earl Gray
D
E
CP
(Verveine citron)

Rom–

A. 1/ Anne Gosh
Tepuca

B. vitello

2. Pousson

C. Pousson (Jusk) (Lagunto)

D. 2. Pasta (Courge / Pumpkin)

E. 3 dessert.

Between the present and the future, why not save time?

Germaine Dulac

COCKTAILS & MORE
RECIPES FROM **PARIS**

FRANCK AUDOUX

New York · Paris · London · Milan

Cravan, in the 16th arrondissement, is a space that reflects Franck's personality – both old and new. It is a warm place where a unique atmosphere reigns, fostering encounters and the emergence of a shared culture. It is a place I deeply love.

Shinichiro Ogata
Designer & founder of Ogata Paris

I first made my way to the 16th some years ago on a recommendation from a friend to check out this great little bar serving very good drinks. What I found was Cravan (and Franck of course), a beautiful bijou of an art nouveau interior with a small zinc bar top, and murals on the ceiling and walls. I immediately thought we found something special, and we did! After a quick introduction to Franck we chatted about cocktails and my love for the Negroni. Without hesitation Franck made me a Tunnel, his riff on the Negroni. Dryer, less sweet, with the addition of white vermouth (Noilly Prat, of course) and served chilled and with a dash of grapefruit. Perfection in a glass I thought! We have been friends ever since.

Matt Hranek
Author and founder/editor of *Wm Brown* Magazine

In conceiving and bringing Cravan to life in 2018, in Paris's sixteenth arrondissement, Franck Audoux placed the cocktail on an unexpected, off-centered axis. He envisions it as timeless – free from its past and origins, free from fixed recipes, free to go and become whatever it desires, wherever it wishes. Its refined taste must reflect the experiences it creates: elegant, precise, singular, even rebellious.

For emancipation lies at its core–just as it did for the Situationists in the 1950s – a form of resurgence. Cravan is a social idea, a gustatory idea, and, as is often the case when venturing across familiar terrain, an avant-garde idea.

Alexandre Gauthier
Chef-owner, La Grenouillère

Cravan is one of those most rare experiences where radical simplicity and profound complexity blend inspiring emotion and intellectual curiosity.

Miren Arzalluz
Director General, Guggenheim Museum Bilbao

With his attention to detail and a focus on flavor, Franck Audoux is the quintessential French barman. He's created, and curated, a pitch-perfect cocktail experience at Cravan in Paris, shaking and stirring seemingly simple ingredients together to create superbly balanced drinks. This collection of stories and recipes will transport you into his wonderful world of cocktails, wherever you are.

David Lebovitz
Author, *Drinking French*

When I first entered the doors of Cravan in the 16th arrondissement, I fell instantly, inexplicably in love. The place, the cocktails, the music, the human warmth – and something more. I immediately wanted to be a part of it. Then I met Franck. I decoded him and helped him bring to life what Cravan is today and what it will become tomorrow. Without certainty, guided by genuine encounters, we are – I believe – creating a unique and fascinating world.

Caroline Grenthe
Director general, Cravan

Preface

Thinking back, it all started in a contemporary art gallery now located near the Place des Vosges, a gallery founded by Michel Rein. It was here, in the mid 1990s that I met talented people, learned to decipher the avant-garde and immersed myself in artistic Paris.

These were fluid, effervescent years that redefined the contours of Parisian cultural life. In 2006, during this exciting period, I had the opportunity to take part alongside Iñaki Aizpitarte, in the Chateaubriand adventure, a restaurant set up in a former old-fashioned bistro on Avenue Parmentier. Together, as a group, and little by little, we imagined a new world. For me, it was an intense ten years, during which terms like "fooding" and "bistronomy" entered our common vocabulary and ultimately led to the revitalization of the east of Paris. To me this all justified the leap from contemporary art to the restaurant business. After training my eyes with Michel Rein, Iñaki Aizpitarte offered me the opportunity to train my palate. I embarked on a trailblazing experience, propelled by a spirit of freedom that was in no small part influenced by seeing the Catalan chef Ferran Adrià, an invited speaker at Documenta in Kassel in 2007.

Chateaubriand was a restaurant project with an ambitious, uninhibited aesthetic. I imagined a new approach to service that was both precise and informal all the while attentive to the guest's needs, because conventions are made to be challenged. Humor, irony and an outsider's perspective all helped us rethink the stifled mindset of a traditional restaurant.

I opened the place to artists, authors, and soon, to the cocktail world. Sensing the rapid evolution of the bar scene abroad, in 2012 I organized a pairing of cocktails and creative cuisine as part of the "In Good Company" soirées we hosted at Le Dauphin, the tapas bar next door to Le Chateaubriand. Thanks to a joint effort between our kitchen and internationally renowned bartenders, we were laying the foundations for "haute gastronomie liquide."

Behind this project was the desire to bring people together to pool ideas, catalyze thought and encourage a group approach. In this, I have not forgotten the meaning of the exhibitions we organized with Michel Rein. I still want to unite talents to give life to new projects, and I continue to reason in terms of addition rather than subtraction, convinced that creative imagination is cumulative.

My hope is that Cravan will continue to forge closer ties, whether through the cocktails themselves, in the combinations of drinks and cuisine we offer, or with the designers with whom we collaborate. I believe in the right kind of encounters.

This is why I like to combine ingredients that are sometimes very powerful. Cravan then becomes a playground for imagining and experimenting with highly original associations, particularly with spirits. Without ever altering them, I seek to reveal them by accentuating their aromas or moving them into other realms of taste. The approach begins with respect for the initial product, then moves on to combinations of ingredients that allow us to taste them fully, and sometimes even rediscover them. I am constantly obsessed with taste, and even more so with balance. Without this perpetual pursuit of the right balance, working on flavors is doomed to fail.

It is the finesse of the tiniest detail that makes the difference. Here, my work approaches the gastronomic repertoire.

Cravan's story and development are a faithful reflection of the connections I form in my mind. Nothing on display or served at Cravan exists without them. Past, present, tradition, avant-garde, music, cinema, fashion, encounters – everything is linked in my mind. At Cravan, there are no ideas without roots, no projects without origins.

We start from the cocktail and its history to offer our creations, as well as to break new ground in areas such as fashion and publishing. I am firmly convinced that there is no room for chance, that every idea must come from a point of reference, that distance plays an essential role, and perspective gives us power. I am always mindful of Pierre Reverdy's words: "The more distant and distinct the relationship between two realities that are brought together, the more powerful the image."

Postface

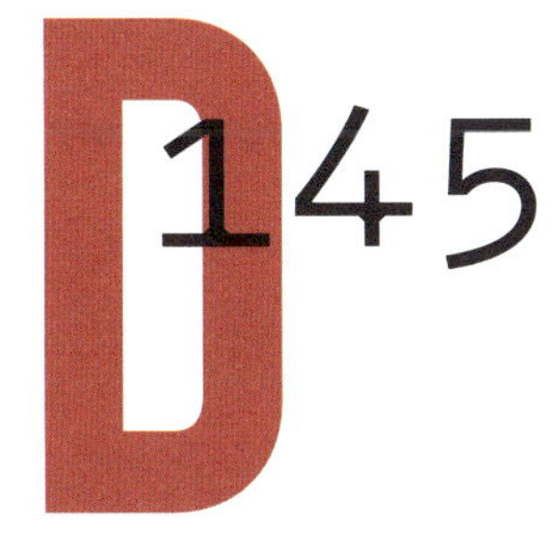

Details

Exception

Food

Jacket

Knockout

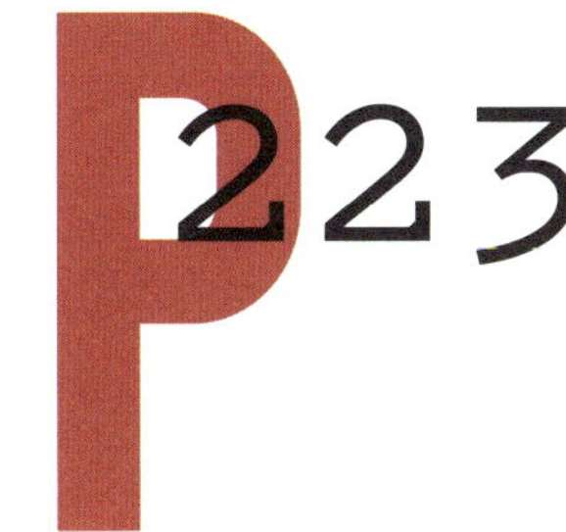

Playlist

Quote

Royal

Very Good

259

Wandering

XO

267

Zest

I have always seen the cocktail not as an end in itself but as the beginning of a story. A story that goes far beyond the drink itself and becomes a mise en abyme (a story within a story). The cocktail is always an open window onto other universes (whether art, gastronomy, literature, fashion, cinema… all my favorite subjects, in short) which, by a mirror effect, tell its story in turn. The drinks we create and serve only find their meaning through reverberation! It is precisely through this refocusing and concentration that the cocktail can finally reveal itself fully.

It is therefore the abécédaire that seems to me the most fitting way to express this reverberation and to best convey our vision of cocktails, of which Cravan is their home. A 17th-century house rising in the heart of the Saint-Germain-des-Prés neighborhood in Paris, it gathers within itself all the meaningful elements that make Cravan what it is: a distinct and singular vision of cocktails served there, of the plates offered alongside them, and of all the literary, musical, and cinematic references that nourish Cravan, each one reflecting and extending what is set before you.

Before becoming a four-story house at 165 Boulevard Saint-Germain, Cravan was a tiny 17-seat bar dating from 1911, designed by Hector Guimard, the master of Art Nouveau, which I opened in 2018 in the 16th arrondissement, far out in western Paris.

This discreet address already carried within it a radical proposition and was already driven by the ambition of placing the cocktail front and center. To achieve this, I did away with all the usual bar artifices (visible bottles, menus with endless descriptions, ostentatious garnishes…). As then, just as today, I served only cocktails – and my creations were already marked by a pronounced sense of purity: few ingredients, particular attention to glassware, and an obsession with balance, taste, and flavor, along with a deliberate simplicity. I like to say that my cocktails are not complicated but complex. An apparent simplicity opening onto a gustatory complexity. In the same way, I lay claim to a certain amateurism – "for one never lives long enough to be anything else!" (Charlie Chaplin) – as a synonym for curiosity. Never forget to perform free figures and gestures during compulsory exercises. Never be content with the rule, but strive toward the exception.

The "little Cravan" turned out to be a prototype, from which the House of Saint-Germain-des-Prés was able to amplify all the correspondences that were born there. At the center of proceedings, then – not on a pedestal, but already as an example of transversality (the most interesting chess piece remains the bishop, after all, since it moves diagonally)! Reverberation, concentration, connection, correspondence, affinity: these are the ways in which we think about the cocktail: above all, since it is the beginning of everything. But it is only in tasting it, and through it, that you can access this creative principle – and, in reverse, be able to savor it fully.

The abécédaire thus allows us to open all these windows[01] and, at the same time, to consider in its entirety what Cravan offers. The alphabet book itself as the form of a chance promenade, without logical continuity, leaping from letter to letter, each one a piece of the same puzzle. And what puzzle is that? The desire to create an art of living of which the cocktail is the point of departure!

01 **Flore Garcin-Marrou**, "L'Abécédaire de Gilles Deleuze," in Art and Alphabet, Ligeia review, no. 153-156, January-June 2017, pp. 212-219.

Alphabet Book / Abécédaire

A

It is my habit, in the evening, to walk along Boulevard Saint-Germain. The day before yesterday I met a friend there. Suddenly the rain began to pour down and we decided to take shelter in a darkened theater. Then came the moment of choosing our seats, and the crucial question: where were we going to sit?

Would we take the front rows, the middle, or the back of the room? As we had known each other for a long time and had nothing left to prove to one another, we immediately ruled out the back rows. I thought of Luc Moullet's film *Les Sièges de l'Alcazar*, which I had seen a few days earlier – "for nothing in the world would I sit in the third row, much less farther back" – when my friend, a cinephile beyond his years, pulled me by the arm:

– Let's sit in the front row.
– Why so close?
– Well, to enter the film, of course, to merge with it, to drown in it!

I refrained from pointing out that in doing so we were missing something essential – the frame. And, knowing his excess, I allowed myself a digression, the only thing I shared with Petrarch, being a talent for such diversions, and asked him:

– And in a cocktail bar, where do you sit?
– Everyone knows the best bars in the world have only three stools. So I sit on one of them. Do you remember Delluc's *L'Homme des Bars*, that shot plunging onto the barman's hands, the only thing illuminated? That's what I'm looking for!

I had no idea what he was talking about.

– And at home? I pressed. You do buy bottled cocktails. Where, then, are the barman's hands?
– For me, you see, the bottled cocktail is to the bar what the DVD is to the cinema. It is already an object, just as the film is one. And through that bottle the barman has passed on his *savoir-faire*. The position in which I drink it is different, and even if I never physically go to that bar, the cocktail allows me to taste that movement, that tension unique to each barman. His style, in short!

– And streaming? I ventured.
– You know, films are like cocktails: there are good ones and bad ones!

At that, the film began, and I fell asleep.

Whisky Mag #82
March 2022

Bring
Cravan Home

COCKTAILS
PRÊTS À SERVIR
CRAVAN
QUINCE
MARGARITA
SERVIR FRAIS
50 CL
BOULEVARDI
COCKTAILS
PRÊTS À SERVIR
CRAVAN
QUINCE
MARGARITA
SERVIR FRAIS
18% VOL.
50 CL

C
C
C
C
C
COCKTAILS
PRÊTS À SERVIR
CRA
NEGRONI
VAN
21% VOL.
SERVIR FRAIS
50 CL
COCKTAILS
PRÊTS À SERVIR
CRA
QUINCE
MARGARITA
VAN
18% VOL.
SERVIR FRAIS
50 CL
COCKTAILS
PRÊTS À SERVIR
CRA
NEGRONI
VAN
21% VOL.
SERVIR FRAIS
50 CL

CRA
VAN
Rivoli
COCKTAILS

Foie Gras de
Canard Entier
CRA
Mina
NAV
COCKTAILS
Negroni
COCKTAILS
CRA
Archi
VAN
COCKTAILS

In conversation with Dominique Païni

C

Cinema

WHEN WILL
YOU STOP MAKING
CINEMA?

WHEN
I START.
JEAN-LUC GODARD

One day, Dominique Païni received a long email from Franck Audoux inviting him to a conversation about cinema and its cultural heritage, programming, and what it means to show people things and therefore reduce them to ruins. The theoretician, critic and exhibition curator replied with a simple “Okay! When?”, committing him to the meeting.

Païni's life was dedicated to “constructing closeness” and thinking about films, including those of Jean-Luc Godard, with whom he rubbed shoulders for about thirty years. Païni evokes how the “seventh art” is a collective act, because “in a movie theater, we see a film and also those who watch the film.” Throughout his career, Païni developed a history of the cinematographic art that he organized and displayed in galleries and museums.

The encounter between the two men took place at Païni's home in the heart of Paris. On one of his shelves adorned with books and souvenirs, his files containing written correspondences with Jean-Luc Godard were missing… On the day of the interview, these famous letters were in the hands of a brave student who was in charge of transcribing them so they could be made into a book. The epistolary exchanges between the two men were lively and gripping, humorous and surprising. Païni has described himself as “a bit of a fetishist” about Godard.

Païni had it in mind to create a new exhibition dedicated to the filmmaker, who passed away on September 13, 2022. He once said to Godard, during a public conference: “I would have been less happy without your films, but having known you hasn't offered me what your films have filled me with in terms of intellectual stimulation and gains in sensibility.” The remark provoked uncomfortable laughter from their entourage. “On that day, he had a marvellous smile. People were saying bad things about him! He so hated devotion,” recounts Païni, who admits: “I am a devotee, Godard being a great artistic genius of the 20th and 21st centuries. And this conviction increases with tireless viewing of the films.” A great admirer of Godardian cinema, Franck Audoux is quite comfortable sharing this opinion.

FA Jacques Rivette said: "The classics are the modern [films] that succeeded," or, depending on the source, "that stood the test of time." Beyond the impact of this quote, which I find impressively efficient, how do we define a classic today?

DP The classics in cinema, in literature, and in the majority of artistic disciplines are frequently works that were not admired in their time. It's their untimeliness, their lack of recognition at the moment of their appearance, which, when we discover them, makes us realize that they weren't recognized as major works. Retrospectively, these works are considered classics upon reevaluation. I can give the example of the film by Robert Bresson, *Four Nights of a Dreamer* (1971). Many of my generation misjudged it. Another film dating from the previous year, just a few months apart, is Michelangelo Antonioni's *Zabriskie Point*, which can be compared to Bresson's film from the point of view of the skepticism and critical reception it received at the time.

The two films deal with the same subject: the hippie phenomenon and the counter-culture of this era. One takes place in the parched conditions of Death Valley in Nevada, the other in the humidity of the banks of the Seine at night. Even though they seem distant, or even opposite, from each other, these two films are very closely related.

Like many filmmakers who didn't bother with formal expressive traits, when they did appropriate one, it became almost literally a didactic appropriation.

In *Zabriskie Point*, there's an amazing sequence that has always fascinated me. If you pay close attention half-way through the film, there's a sequence that confronts something the filmmaker ignored throughout his work: the intense experience of the sublime. All of a sudden, the director – who was radical in his "minimalist" effects – decided to reflect upon a certain romantic lyricism. This sequence is the most lyrical in the film: the staging creates an elevation of the characters, conferring upon them an angelic status. And yet he – the modern artist par excellence, who doesn't look backwards towards subjects related to the culture of the past was the only artist who, along with Godard, made no films using historic costumes.

Zabriskie Point and *Four Nights of a Dreamer* are films which we didn't treat kindly in their time. People thought that the two filmmakers were beginning to age. Bresson was almost 70, and was filming what I believe to be one of the most beautiful nudes in cinema, as we might say in painting or in sculpture. The camera caresses the body of a young woman (Isabelle Weingarten) without any erotic effect. It's a nude painted by the movement of the camera. These two films have become, fifty years later, immense classics.
The final scene in *Zabriskie Point* – the famous sequence filmed with a camera that recorded at over 5000 images per second – the explosion of a villa in slow-motion with music by Pink Floyd, recalls all the iconography of Pop Art, with these mass market food products filling American apartments, which are the stereotypes of comfort. All of these objects explode and fly away against a neutral background. Slow motion is the effect of the sublime in cinema. In short, these two films are immense classics!

A great classic will appear as such, including through the culpability of critics who admit having "passed it by." To come back to Rivette's catchphrase, *The Rules of the Game* by Jean Renoir (1939) is a classic par excellence. It's a film that was shortened through various mutilating interventions. A considerable number of great classics are films that were not initially recognized as such.

FA Franck Audoux
DP Dominique Païni
MO Marie Ottavi

THE CLASSICS ARE THE MODERN THAT SUCCEEDED.

JACQUES RIVETTE

FA Hence the importance of time. So, is time necessary for understanding these films?

DP Yes and no. For example, *Drive My Car* by Ryūsuke Hamaguchi and *Misericordia* by Alain Guiraudie were perceived as future classics from the moment they appeared.

FA If I make reference to cocktails, a classic is a recipe imagined by others in another time which interests me through how it speaks to me gustatively today, and thereby incites me to work based on what I've learned. What do classics, such as we've just defined them, have to offer?

DP They offer contradictory things, just as a cocktail sometimes contains. Your reference might make people smile, but I think, on the contrary, that intellectual things are not without relation to gustative phenomena.

The classics were appropriate propositions for their day, but they weren't always noticed. They reflect the world in which they were produced. The work of art reflects a spirit of the times that's translated more formally than through the realism of recounted anecdotes. In this respect, the film, as a work of art, becomes a classic with good reason. What we call a classic is that which leaves a legacy of codes for works to come. *Breathless*, the first film by Godard, was indigestible for some but it "imposed" the codes of storytelling for the future. A large part of the cinema that would follow, from 1960 until today, including advertising films, borrows from the narrative codes and the direct addressing of the audience inherited from the New Wave. At the time, we had every reason to want to project ourselves as the character Michel Poiccard, played by Jean-Paul Belmondo, or Antoine Doinel from Truffaut's *The 400 Blows*… Poiccard turns towards us and hurls "fuck off" from behind the wheel of his car, and Doinel turns towards us in the film's final freeze-frame shot.

In 1965, when I saw *Pierrot le Fou*, my life changed. I tried to identify with many aspects of what Belmondo's character, Pierrot/Ferdinand, experiences. But the fiction is disturbed by interruptions from outside of the story, which prevented me from having a total imaginary projection into the character.

A cocktail is the mix, the confrontation, the hybridization of labilities and "effervescences", of acidities, bitternesses, sweetness… It's a drink that "flows" from a "program." Thinking about it the "right" way doesn't mean bringing together things that resemble each other. Nor do gustative proximities necessarily make a good cocktail. It's also about oppositions, things that risk being explosive!

The cocktail is a way of confronting things that have no reason to be associated, the art of montage. It's also about making things disappear, no longer thinking about them, dissolving them and bringing them back. To know is to recognize.

FA Jean Douchet liked to say that he showed films that had been seen without ever having been watched. Through your experience at Studio 43, the theater you ran, how important is programming? What are the issues at stake in program selection?

DP We could just as well say the contrary: films that were watched without ever having been seen! But the two formulations suggest the same thing! Programming is really creating a mix and demonstrating a non dogmatic approach. Jean Douchet, for example, had very distinct tastes. I was always amazed by the way he hosted cinema clubs with films that I couldn't see how he could link together, which were chosen just as much for his own pleasure and intellectual interest. I once claimed the freedom to like a film made by a filmmaker whose overall work I don't care for. Programming is also about thinking contrary to oneself. When one takes the risk of being a programmer, one is supposed to assume and then "exhaust" one's own taste. You have to show and share things that don't speak to you aesthetically. For me, programming is a fecund danger, a fertile risk that you might change your mind about films and works of art. Films are time-objects. The material of cinema is time. It's not just visual, but rather an experience that is lived through time.

MO Do you follow certain programming rules?

DP I feel very much like a shopkeeper, a little (luxury!) grocer. I am a cinema connoisseur, that's undeniable, and it was part of my career, but I'm also someone who "sells." *The Rise and Fall of a Small Film Company* is the title of an art-house film by Godard from 1986…

My programming features films that attract seasoned cinephiles. When I'm working on a program, I try to combine very serious films that aren't entertaining or attractive with films whose proximity in the program "colors" the former with unexpected interpretive hypotheses, or, on the contrary, gives gravity to films with futile ambitions. I want to bring together resemblances that cry out, clamorous similarities. The gravity of a work by Molière is equal to the burlesque of a work by Shakespeare. I'm not sure that we are moved to pity when Molière tries to make us identify with pain. We have to attempt with films what you attempt with cocktails.

FA If we accept Henri Langlois' idea that the most beautiful films are those we have not yet seen, can programming claim to "show" a history of cinema?

DP There are two responses.

There was a time when it was possible to make a history of cinema with the feeling that we could do it easily and completely, from the earliest films to modern cinema. We had the feeling that we had "seen it all" and discussed everything that was accessible. Many films were lost (momentarily). And we lacked the funds to restore them. Frequently, they were destroyed by the producers or forgotten within catalogues that had been bought out by industrial groups. There were copies dispersed in unknown places. When we started to more seriously seek out the lost and forgotten films as of the 1980s, it was possible to make a fresh history of cinema that extended those that the first historians – Henri Fescourt, Georges Sadoul, Jean Mitry and many others – had provisionally concluded.

The second response is that in cinema - as they say in painting or in the history of any kind of art – in the 1960s we were still in the incredible position of shaking hands with the greats of early cinema: Walsh, Hawks, Ford… As if twentieth-century art historians had been able to shake hands with Picasso and Giotto. A first history of cinema was accomplished at the time when many artists from the history of this art were still alive, and according to a historiographic model conforming to an organic outline copied from human existence: birth (the invention of the medium and the "pioneers," the "first" filmmakers, classicism (the affirmation of codes relating to direction, editing and dramaturgy imported from nineteenth-century novels, in a nutshell), a mannerist academicism (filmmakers codify and fix classicism in an "intangible manner"), modernity (models are borrowed in cinemas just as modern painters interpret the old masters; cinema becomes the subject of films). This reductivist summary off the top of my head is only to give the sense that the history of cinema takes place within about a hundred years, while that of the fine arts takes place over five hundred years, from the Renaissance of the 15th century to the late 19th century, the "Belle Epoque," which saw the appearance of animated photography.

Today, with digital technology, film production has exploded. There are thousands of films to consult for the people who must select them at the International Film Festival in Cannes. In Paris, the number of new films that appear weekly in cinemas is very high!

FA Can we consider that the digital might be the museographic tool of cinema? Jean-Luc Godard said that the DVD and then digital technology allowed for its archaeology. What do you think about this?

DA The fact that DVDs still exist is a sign that many people want films to be embodied in a library object. There is something noble about having a DVD collection, sometimes arranged near the books on our shelves. My DVDs are mixed in with my books, or at least very close to them. I like the DVD because it's less "sterilized"; it still retains a bit of the "grain" that blu-ray definitively erased. And the DVD allows us to make excerpts of films and to study a sequence in the same way one studies a chapter from a book. We can only study a film if we "cut it up", only if we study it based on the details in the excerpts. Just as we visually and photographically "cut" a painting. The excerpts allow us to compare films. The appreciation of the latter, their analysis, is only possible through this visual and intellectual undertaking of comparison. There is no history of the art without confronting and comparing the styles of filmmakers. The history of an art cannot ignore aesthetic study. But this history is only possible through the ability to reproduce films as photography can reproduce paintings, sculptures and works of architecture. Reproduction allows for the study of works of fine art through comparison, with photographs passing from one historian to the next. Photographic reproductions and videographic reproductions of films have allowed for art historians to have "imaginary museums". That said, I need to see films at the cinema, just as I concentrate more easily reading in a library: you read a book, and you immediately want to read another because research obviously increases one's sources of erudition and knowledge. It's the combination of books that is the foundation of our culture, just as the combination of alcohols in a cocktail creates new and subtle flavors!

SHOW
WHAT EVERYONE
HAS SEEN

BUT NOT
WATCHED.

JEAN DOUCHET

Jean-Luc
GODARD
introduction à une véritable
HISTOIRE DU CINEMA
collection ça cinéma
tome 1
Albatros

Image on the left **Jean-Luc Godard**
Introduction to a True History of Cinema.
Albatros Editions, 1980.

GIVING NEW GENERATIONS ACCESS TO FILMS FROM WORLD CINEMA, REGARDLESS OF STYLES OR TECHNICAL DIFFICULTIES. THIS HAS A NAME: PROGRAMMING

FA In your book *Le Musée imaginaire d'Henri Langlois (The Imaginary Museum of Henri Langlois)*, you write: "Giving new generations access to films from world cinema, regardless of styles or technical difficulties. This has a name: programming." Here, we're touching upon the question of transmission. To program is obviously to transmit. What is the importance of transmission?

DP It is to transmit the importance of a work of art: the way it proposes a formal organization of sounds, noises, colors, speeds of things in movement in reality… A work of art doesn't have any expectations of us. If it is reduced to being in the service of an ideology or of gestures that go against the fundamental principles of human existence, its virtue, its legitimacy and its posterity are devalued.

I am wary of the sometimes discreet means employed by capitalism to destroy curiosity. Capitalism irresistibly financializes works of art and erodes our curiosity. This economic and social system, more resistant than any other in modern human history, is founded upon consumption, its fanatical desire if consumption is denied, the accumulation of the symbol and the equivalent of power, which is money. Intellectual work and sharpened criticism are stifled by industrial and political enterprises that threaten democracy.

For example, Gus Van Sant's film *To Die For* (1995) was very underestimated when it was released, and you have to watch it again today. It has become a classic because, in hindsight, we realize that the same year, Paul Verhoeven made a film about a related subject: *Show Girls*. That is to say that it's also trends in cinema that reveal certain films, which confer upon them paradoxical classic status. They bear witness to an era, and the programming task will be to hierarchize the aesthetic success of the films, whose subject matter is not the sole criteria for evaluating their quality.

Everything was done by the capitalist film industry in Hollywood to make these movies a commercial success, but industrial production devalues critical and evaluative activity. The critical exercise happens quickly and considers it a waste of time to analyze these films, therefore depriving itself of gaining a point of view that benefits a cultural anthropology of images. And yet this is the vocation of programming.

A certain number of works from within the consumer film industry are disdained as a result of the effects and consequences of mass production. The critical spirit and aesthetic and semiotic analysis are considerably undermined today by the reduced freedom of judgement caused by social media. The latter have imposed consumption and the misleading illusion that the validity of each person's judgement was a social and humanist ideal, substituting an ideal based on the authority of masters and skills. Transmission is not the only role of programming. It maintains the relevance of works of art, the most sublime of which are those that appear untarnishably capable of "withstanding" the succession of tragedies in the world. We cannot ask more from a work of art than to help us coexist with the worst. In short, to alleviate our pain and our scars. I won't deny that sometimes, the minutes spent savoring the flavor or the delicious giddiness of a cocktail have had this same, albeit fleeting, virtue. But a film is also short-lived!

Methodology

A) **Guiding Principle**
Work around a single ingredient (bitter orange…) or a specific flavor (bitterness…).
Build horizontally.
Strive for balance and tension.

B) **Champagnes and Spirits**
Subtly take the product into new territory.
Enhance and elevate its aromatic profile to push it further.
Lead the spirit toward a new aromatic territory.
Respect the liquid - never distort its essence.

C) **Aromatic Composition**
Approach it like crafting a perfume; a pronounced, expressive nose.

D) **Classics**
Adapt and modernize.
Give classics a fresh perspective without losing their essence.

C

Cocktails

ROYAL BASILIC

Champagne Brut .... 100ml | 3½fl oz
Basil infusion .... 2.5ml | ½tsp

Pour the Champagne into a chilled coupe and add the infusion. Gently stir to combine.

BASIL INFUSION

Dry basil flowers .... 4g | 1tsp
Superfine sugar .... 125g | 4½oz
Filtered water .... 500ml | 17fl oz

Place basil flowers and sugar in a heatproof container. Heat the water to 100°C | 212°F and pour over the mix. Stir lightly to combine. Cover with plastic wrap and infuse for 40 minutes. Double strain and allow to cool.

Through a delicate infusion focused on vegetable elements (leaves, seeds, and herbs), with no added alcohol and little to no sugar, Champagne reveals another side of itself. The infusion does not hide its character but refines it, bringing forward its nuance and length.

This is the essence of Le Royal: a meeting of clarity, restraint, and precision. Royal Basilic is the first recipe we created and have been serving since the founding of Cravan.

FRENCH 75

- Agastache gin .... 30ml | 1fl oz
- Simple syrup .... 15ml | ½fl oz
- Fresh lemon juice .... 15ml | ½fl oz
- Absinthe .... 1 dash
- Champagne brut .... top
- Lemon twist

Combine all the ingredients except Champagne in a shaker with ice. Hard shake for two seconds. Double strain into a chilled coupe. Top with Champagne. Gently stir to combine. Discard lemon twist.

AGASTACHE GIN

- Dried agastache flowers*............ 5g | 1¾tsp
- London dry gin .... 700g | 24fl oz

**anise hyssop*

Infuse the ingredients in an airtight container and refrigerate for 24 hours. Strain and then filter the gin through a premoistened paper filter. Store refrigerated.

SIMPLE SYRUP

- Superfine sugar .... 100g | 3½oz
- Filtered water .... 100ml | 3½fl oz

Place the sugar in a heatproof container. Pour the water over the sugar. Stir until fully dissolved. Refrigerate until chilled.

ALFONSO

Orange, Bitters, Wein FMK .... 20ml | ⅔fl oz
Simple syrup .... 1.25ml | ¼tsp
Bitter orange .... 2 dashes
Champagne brut rosé .... 120ml | 4fl oz
Orange twist

Put all the ingredients into a chilled flute, finishing with Champagne. Gently stir to combine. Discard orange twist.

SIMPLE SYRUP See page 70.

Orange, Bitters, Wein FMK is a red oxydative wine-based aperitif with orange notes and an aromatic bitters aroma I created with Freimeisterkollektiv, an alliance of independent craft distillers and leading bartenders.

The term *Freimeister* draws from a tradition of exceptional European craftsmen, freed from guild rules for their skill – archetypes of the modern artist, following their own path with courage and mastery. Today, the lone artisan cannot thrive in a spirits market dominated by global corporations; true distinction requires both craft and platforms that amplify one's voice. The *Freimeisterkollektiv* serves as this stage: each distiller, bartender, and creative partner brings a unique style, yet only through exchange and collaboration does a product transcend the individual. A paradox emerges: each *Freimeister* remains autonomous, producing distinctive work, while contributing to a network greater than the sum of its parts. The project's potential lies in this tension – the dynamic interplay of individual mastery and collective empowerment. Freimesterkollektiv is based in Berlin.

ROSSINI

Rhubarb cordial .... 25ml | ¾fl oz
Strawberry-infused vodka ...... 20ml | ⅔fl oz
Champagne brut .... 50ml | 1¾fl oz

Stir the cordial and vodka in a stainless steel mixing tin with ice for 20 seconds. Double strain into a chilled coupe glass. Add Champagne and stir gently.

RHUBARB CORDIAL

Superfine sugar .... 100g | 3½oz
Rhubarb juice .... 250ml | 8fl oz
Tartaric acid .... 0.5g | ⅛tsp

Press rhubarb with a cold-press juicer. Filter through a Superbag. Dissolve sugar in the filtered rhubarb juice. Add tartaric acid and stir until fully dissolved.

STRAWBERRY-INFUSED VODKA

Strawberries (Anaïs variety) ..... 250g | 9oz
Vodka .... 700ml | 24fl oz
Simple syrup .... 10ml | 2tsp

Wash, hull, and halve the strawberries. Place in a vacuum-seal bag with the vodka. Vacuum-seal and cook sous-vide at 52°C | 125.6°F for 1 hour. Strain through a sieve. Refrigerate until ready to use.

SIMPLE SYRUP See page 70.

DRY MARTINI

Dolin dry vermouth .... 30ml | 1fl oz
London dry gin .... 30ml | 1fl oz
Nocellara olive (natural)

Stir with ice in a stainless steel mixing tin for 12 seconds. Double strain into a chilled coupe glass. Garnish with the olive.

Our martinis are mixed in equal parts, offering a less alcoholic cocktail with greater aromatic expression.

DIRTY MARTINI

Noilly Prat dry vermouth........ 30ml | 1fl oz
Olive oil-infused vodka .... 30ml | 1fl oz
Olive brine .... 2.5ml | ½tsp
Olive tincture .... 1.25ml | ¼tsp
Nocellara olive (natural)

Stir the vermouth and vodka with ice in a stainless steel mixing tin for 12 seconds. Double strain into a chilled coupe glass. Add the olive brine and stir gently. Garnish with the olive. Add the olive tincture just before serving.

OLIVE OIL-INFUSED VODKA

Vodka .... 100ml | 3½fl oz
Nocellara olive oil .... 2 drops

Place vodka and olive oil in a vacuum-seal bag. Vacuum-seal and cook sous-vide at 60°C | 140°F for 30 minutes. Stop the cooking by plunging the bag into an ice bath. Filter through a premoistened paper filter. Refrigerate until ready to use.

OLIVE TINCTURE

Nocellara olive (natural) .... 4g | 1tsp
96% neutral alcohol .... 10ml | ⅓fl oz

Place olive and alcohol into a vacuum-seal bag. Vacuum-seal and cook sous-vide at 60°C | 140°F for 60 minutes. Stop the cooking by plunging the bag into an ice bath. Filter through a premoistened paper filter. Refrigerate until ready to use.

XERÈS MARTINI

London dry gin .... 30ml | 1fl oz
Dolin dry vermouth .... 30ml | 1fl oz
Palo Cortado sherry .... 10ml | ⅓fl oz
Nocellara olive (natural)

Stir the gin, vermouth, and sherry with ice in a stainless steel mixing tin for 12 seconds. Double strain into a chilled coupe glass. Garnish with the Nocellara olive.

GIBSON

London dry gin .... 30ml | 1fl oz
Dolin dry vermouth .... 30ml | 1fl oz
Pickle brine .... 1.25ml | ¼tsp
Pickled onion petal .... 1 (for garnish)

Stir gin and vermouth with ice in a stainless steel mixing tin for 12 seconds. Double strain into a chilled coupe glass. Garnish with the pickled onion petal. Pour the pickle brine over the top just before serving.

PICKLED ONION PETALS

Filtered water .... 300ml | 10fl oz
Cider vinegar .... 200ml | 7fl oz
Superfine sugar .... 100g | 3½oz
Onion petals .... 1 onion

Combine water, vinegar, and sugar in a container. Fill until the onion petals are just covered and use for pickling as needed.

VESPER

London dry gin	20ml | ⅔fl oz
Vodka	10ml | ⅓fl oz
Quinine-infused white Lillet	30ml | 1fl oz

Stir all ingredients with ice in a stainless steel mixing tin for 12 seconds. Double strain into a chilled coupe glass.

QUININE-INFUSED WHITE LILLET

Lillet white	120ml | 4fl oz
Red quinine	2g | ½tsp

Combine all ingredients and infuse for 20 minutes. Strain and refrigerate until ready to use.

COCO CAVIAR

Coconut vodka .... 40ml | 1⅓fl oz
Coconut water .... 20ml | ⅔fl oz
Caviar tincture .... 1 drop

Stir the vodka and coconut water with ice in a stainless steel mixing tin for 12 seconds. Double strain into a chilled coupe glass. Add the caviar tincture just before serving.

COCONUT VODKA

Organic coconut oil .... 5ml | 1tsp
Vodka .... 200ml | 7fl oz

Combine the ingredients in a vacuum-seal bag. Vacuum-seal and cook sous-vide at 60°C | 140°F for 30 minutes. Stop the cooking by plunging the bag into an ice bath. Filter through a premoistened paper filter. Refrigerate until ready to use.

CAVIAR TINCTURE

Caviar .... 3g | 1tsp
96% neutral alcohol .... 10ml | ⅓fl oz

Combine the ingredients in a vacuum-seal bag. Vacuum-seal and cook sous-vide at 60°C | 140°F for 1 hour. Stop the cooking by plunging the bag into an ice bath. Filter through a premoistened paper filter.

This recipe draws direct inspiration from one of Albert Adria's creations served at his restaurant Enigma in Barcelona. Here, I wanted to reinterpret his pairing, which he serves in a glass, into a single-liquid composition.

NEGRONI

London dry gin	30ml | 1fl oz
Noilly Prat dry vermouth	30ml | 1fl oz
Campari	20ml | ⅔fl oz
Punt e Mes	10ml | ⅓fl oz
Grapefruit twist	

Stir all ingredients in a stainless steel mixing tin for 4 seconds. Strain into a chilled aperitif glass. Discard grapefruit twist.

BOULEVARDIER

Cognac VS .... 30ml | 1fl oz
Orange, Bitters, Wein FMK ..... 30ml | 1fl oz
Campari .... 20ml | ⅔fl oz

Stir all ingredients with ice in a stainless steel mixing tin for 12 seconds. Double strain into a chilled Old-Fashioned glass.

BIRNE

Fortified pear wine* .... 50ml | 1¾fl oz
Pear cider cordial .... 15ml | ½fl oz
Palo Cortado sherry .... 7.5ml | ¼fl oz
**from Freimeisterkollektiv*

Stir all ingredients with ice in a stainless steel mixing tin for 2 seconds. Strain into a chilled Gimlet glass.

PEAR CIDER CORDIAL

Pear cider .... 750ml | 25fl oz
Superfine sugar .... 125g | 4½oz
Tartaric acid .... 1g | ¼tsp

Bring the pear cider to a boil. Once boiling, reduce the heat and bring to a simmer. Simmer for 5 minutes to reduce slightly. Add sugar and tartaric acid and stir until fully dissolved. Refrigerate until ready to use.

The main ingredient of this cocktail is the pear: its flavor, its texture. The fortified pear wine (from FMK / Freimeisterkollektiv) is paired with the sweetness of the pear cider reduction extended by the oxidative notes of sherry.

AMERICANO

Campari .... 35ml | 1¼fl oz
Punt e Mes .... 35ml | 1¼fl oz
Soda water .... top
Orange wedge

Pour Campari and Punt e Mes in a glass with ice. Stir for 10 seconds. Top with soda water and gently stir to combine. Garnish with the orange wedge.

TROCADERO

Orange, Bitters, Wein FMK .... 75ml | 2½fl oz
Soda water .... 50ml | 1¾fl oz
Orange slices

Stir Orange, Bitters, Wein with ice in a stainless steel mixing tin for 10 seconds. Strain into a highball glass. Top with soda water and stir gently. Garnish with orange slices.

My interpretation of the Spritz.

TROCA CHAUD

Orange, Bitters, Wein FMK ..... 75ml | 2½fl oz
Water (100°C | 212°F) .... 60ml | 2fl oz

Pour the Orange, Bitters, Wein and boiling water in order into a heatproof flute. Express an orange peel over the surface before serving.

MAD COLLINS

London dry gin	30ml | 1fl oz
Fresh lemon juice	30ml | 1fl oz
Ginger syrup	25ml | ¾fl oz
Soda water	top

Pour gin, ginger syrup, and lemon juice into a highball glass with ice. Stir for 10 seconds. Top with soda water and stir gently.

GINGER SYRUP

Fresh ginger juice	200ml | 3½fl oz
Superfine sugar	300g | 5oz

Press fresh ginger using a cold-press juicer and strain (you should have 200ml | 3½fl oz). Whisk with sugar until fully dissolved. Refrigerate until ready to use.

ANNIE

Agastache gin .... 30ml | 1fl oz
Fresh lemon juice .... 15ml | ½fl oz
Star anise syrup .... 15ml | ½fl oz
Filtered water .... 50ml | 1¾fl oz

Combine gin, lemon juice, and syrup in a stainless steel mixing tin with ice. Stir for 10 seconds. Top with the water and stir gently.

AGASTACHE GIN

London dry gin .... 700ml | 24fl oz
Dried agastache flowers* .... 5g | 1¾tsp
**anise hyssop*

Infuse the ingredients in an airtight container and refrigerate for 24 hours. Strain and then filter the gin through a premoistened paper filter. Store refrigerated.

STAR ANISE SYRUP

Star anise .... 5g | 1¾tsp
Superfine sugar .... 120g | 4oz
Filtered water .... 120ml | 4fl oz

Bring the water to 100°C | 212°F, then pour it into a heatproof bowl with the sugar and star anise. Stir until sugar dissolves. Infuse for 10 minutes. Strain and refrigerate until ready to use.

I wanted to create an anise drink without the heaviness of alcohol and sugar. So I turned to agastache flowers, whose sweet anise notes combined with the star anise bring all the freshness I was looking for.

LUCO

Lemon balm vodka .... 40ml | 1⅓fl oz
Nettle syrup .... 15ml | ½fl oz
Fresh lemon juice .... 10ml | ⅓fl oz
Soda water .... top

Combine the vodka, syrup, and juice in a highball glass with ice. Stir for 10 seconds. Top with soda water and stir gently.

LEMON BALM VODKA

Vodka .... 700ml | 24fl oz
Dry lemon balm leaves .... 15g | ½oz

Place ingredients in an airtight container and refrigerate for 24 hours. Filter through a premoistened paper filter. Refrigerate until ready to use.

NETTLE SYRUP

Dried nettles .... 10g | ¼oz
Superfine sugar .... 120g | 4oz
Filtered water .... 120ml | 4fl oz

Bring the water to 100°C | 212°F then pour it into a heatproof bowl with the sugar and dried nettles. Stir until sugar dissolves. Cover with plastic wrap and infuse for 10 minutes. Strain and refrigerate until ready to use.

The plant world is an infinite playground. Much like what we can now experience in contemporary cuisine, I'm thinking here of chef Romain Meder and the philosophy of naturalité envisioned by Alain Ducasse, which opens up a limitless field of expression. Playing with seeds, leaves, and flowers allows me to express, with even greater simplicity, what a cocktail must ultimately embody: its singularity – and, therefore, the complexity of its taste.

CAMBON

Manzanilla sherry .... 50ml | 1¾fl oz
Caper juice .... 2.5ml | ½tsp
Tonic water .... top

Pour Manzanilla sherry in a glass with ice. Stir for 10 seconds. Top with tonic water and stir gently. Add the caper juice and stir again before serving.

APPLE & RHUBARB

Rhubarb vodka .... 40ml | 1⅓fl oz
Rhubarb cordial .... 40ml | 1⅓fl oz
Brut apple cider .... 50ml | 1¾fl oz
Rhubarb shrub .... 5ml | 1tsp

Pour vodka and cordial in a highball glass with ice. Stir gently. Add cider and stir up and down. Float the rhubarb shrub on top.

RHUBARB VODKA

Rhubarb .... 250g | 9oz
Vodka .... 350ml | 12fl oz

Wash, peel, and slice rhubarb. Vacuum-seal with the vodka. Cook sous-vide at 52°C | 125.6°F for 1 hour. Strain through a sieve and then a Superbag.

RHUBARB CORDIAL

Rhubarb juice .... 250ml | 8fl oz
Superfine sugar .... 100g | 3½oz
Tartaric acid .... 0.5g | ⅛tsp

Press rhubarb with a cold-press juicer. Filter through a Superbag (you should have 250ml | 8fl oz). Dissolve sugar in the filtered rhubarb juice. Add tartaric acid and stir until fully dissolved.

RHUBARB SHRUB

Rhubarb .... 250g | 9oz
Superfine sugar .... 150g | 5oz
Filtered water .... 100ml | 3½fl oz
Rhubarb vinegar .... 30ml | 1fl oz

Wash, peel, and slice rhubarb. Combine all ingredients in a vacuum-seal bag. Vacuum-seal and macerate for 5 days at room temperature. Filter through a Superbag and refrigerate until ready to use.

PALOMA

Timur berry tequila .... 40ml | 1⅓fl oz
Grapefruit cordial .... 40ml | 1⅓fl oz
Fresh lime juice .... 5ml | 1tsp
Tonic water .... top
Grapefruit wedge

Pour cordial, tequila, and lime juice in a glass with ice. Stir for 15 seconds. Top with tonic water and stir gently. Garnish with a grapefruit wedge.

GRAPEFRUIT CORDIAL

Grapefruit juice .... 250ml | 8fl oz
Superfine sugar .... 90g | 3¼oz
Grapefruit zest .... 10g | ¾oz
Malic acid .... 0.5g | ⅛tsp

Macerate sugar and zest for 5 minutes, until sugar takes on color. Cover and infuse for 2 hours. Filter grapefruit juice. Add juice to sugar and stir until sugar fully dissolved. Filter again, add malic acid, and stir. Refrigerate until ready to use.

TIMUR BERRY TEQUILA

Tequila blanco .... 200ml | 7fl oz
Timur berries .... a pinch

Grind berries into powder. Vacuum-seal with the tequila. Cook sous-vide at 52°C | 125.6°F for 20 minutes. Stop the cooking by plunging the bag into an ice bath. Filter through a premoistened paper filter. Refrigerate until ready to use.

BLOODY MARY

Vodka .... 40ml | 1⅓fl oz
Fresh lemon juice .... 15ml | ½fl oz
Tomato mix .... top
Lemon wedge

Pour vodka and lemon juice in a highball glass with ice. Stir for 10 seconds. Top with tomato mix and stir gently. Garnish with a lemon wedge.

TOMATO MIX

Tomato juice .... 1l | 34fl oz
Passata .... 700g | 24½oz
Worcestershire sauce .... 150ml | 5fl oz
Soy sauce .... 45ml | 1½fl oz
Homemade spicy vinegar .... 30ml | 1fl oz
Smoked salt .... 2.5g | 1tsp

Whisk all ingredients together. Store in an airtight container in the refrigerator until ready to use.

HOMEMADE SPICY VINEGAR

Malt vinegar .... 200ml | 7fl oz
Pili pili chili .... 20g | ¾oz
Maldon salt .... 10g | ¼oz

Combine ingredients in an airtight container. Infuse at room temperature for 5 days. Filter and bottle. Refrigerate until ready to use.

VIRGIN MARY

Omit the vodka.

ZAN

Agastache syrup .... 15ml | ½fl oz
Fresh lemon juice .... 15ml | ½fl oz
Star anise soda .... top

Pour syrup and lemon juice in a glass with ice. Stir for 10 seconds. Top with soda and stir gently.

AGASTACHE SYRUP

Dried agastache* flowers .... 2g | ½tsp
Superfine sugar .... 120g | 4oz
Filtered water .... 120ml | 4fl oz
anise hyssop

Pour boiling water (100°C | 212°F) into a heatproof bowl with the sugar and agastache. Stir until sugar dissolves. Infuse for 7 minutes. Filter and refrigerate until ready to use.

STAR ANISE SODA

Filtered water .... 1l | 34fl oz
Star anise .... 20g | ¾oz

Pour boiling water (100°C | 212°F) into a heatproof bowl with the star anise. Infuse for 20 minutes. Filter and refrigerate until ready to use. Pour into a siphon and charge with one gas cartridge before use.

GINGER

Fresh lemon juice .... 30ml | 1fl oz
Ginger syrup .... 25ml | ¾fl oz
Soda water .... top

Pour syrup and lemon juice in a highball glass with ice. Stir for 10 seconds. Top with soda water and stir gently.

GINGER SYRUP

Fresh ginger juice .... 100ml | 3½fl oz
Superfine sugar .... 150g | 5oz

Press fresh ginger using a cold-press juicer and strain (you should have 100ml | 3½fl oz). Whisk juice and sugar together until sugar is fully dissolved. Refrigerate until ready to use.

I didn't want to create yet another ginger ale or ginger beer but a cocktail that truly embodies the essence of ginger. This drink is a long, vibrant shot alive with spice and the raw energy of the root itself.

TUILERIES

Nettle cordial .... 75ml | 2½fl oz
Lemon balm soda .... 100ml | 3½fl oz

Pour the cordial into a highball glass over ice. Stir for 10 seconds. Add the soda and stir gently again.

NETTLE CORDIAL

Filtered water .... 600ml | 20fl oz
Superfine sugar .... 175g | 6oz
Dried nettles .... 10g | ¼oz
Tartaric acid .... 3g | 1tsp

Bring the water to 100°C | 212°F then pour it into a heatproof bowl with the sugar and dried nettles. Add the acid. Stir until sugar and acid dissolves. Infuse for 10 minutes. Strain and refrigerate until ready to use.

LEMON BALM SODA

Filtered water .... 1l | 34fl oz
Dry lemon balm leaves .... 25g | 1oz

Bring the water to 100°C | 212°F, then pour it into a heatproof bowl with the lemon balm. Stir and infuse for 5 minutes. Strain and refrigerate until ready to use. Pour into a siphon and charge with one gas cartridge before use.

OYSTER TONIC

Oyster infusion .... 60ml | 2fl oz
Caper juice .... 1.25ml | ¼tsp
Tonic water .... top

Build over ice in a highball glass. Top infusion with tonic water and stir gently. Add the caper juice.

OYSTER INFUSION

Fresh oyster leaves .... 15g | ½oz
Filtered water .... 120ml | 4fl oz

Roughly chop the oyster leaves and infuse in the water for 15 minutes. Strain and refrigerate until ready to use.

MERLIMONT

Dry basil flower cordial ..... 50ml | 1¾fl oz
White Kampot pepper soda .... top

Build over ice in a highball glass. Top cordial with soda and stir gently.

DRY BASIL FLOWER CORDIAL

Filtered water .... 300ml | 10fl oz
Extra fine white sugar .... 75g | 2½oz
Dried basil flowers .... 4g | 1tsp
Tartaric acid .... 1g | ¼tsp

Bring the water to 100°C | 212°F then pour it into a heatproof bowl with the sugar and basil flowers. Add the acid. Stir until sugar and acid dissolve. Infuse for 10 minutes. Strain and refrigerate until ready to use.

WHITE KAMPOT PEPPER SODA

Filtered water .... 500ml | 17fl oz
White kampot pepper .... 0.5g | ⅛tsp

Bring the water to 100°C | 212°F then pour it into a heatproof bowl with the pepper and infuse for 10 minutes. Strain and refrigerate until ready to use. Pour into a siphon and charge with one gas cartridge before use.

This cocktail was created for a cocktail-pairing dinner with Alexandre Gauthier, the two-Michelin-star chef of La Grenouillère. It pays homage to the location of one of his other restaurants, Sur Mer, and the cuisine reflects simplicity and perfect balance.

TOMMY'S MARGARITA

Tequila blanco .... 50ml | 1¾fl oz
Fresh lime juice .... 25ml | ¾fl oz
Agave syrup .... 10ml | ⅓fl oz

Combine all ingredients in a shaker with ice. Shake for 12 seconds. Double strain into a chilled Gimlet glass.

ELDERFLOWER MARGARITA

Tequila blanco .... 30ml | 1fl oz
Elderflower liqueur .... 25ml | ¾fl oz
Fresh lemon juice .... 5ml | 1tsp

Stir for 25 seconds in a stainless steel mixing tin with ice. Double strain into a chilled Gimlet glass.

CAMPAGNE PREMIÈRE

Lemon-infused vodka .... 40ml | 1⅓fl oz
Egg white .... 25ml | ¾fl oz
Fresh lemon juice .... 20ml | ⅔fl oz
Lemon verbena syrup .... 15ml | ½fl oz

Combine ingredients in a shaker without ice. Shake for 8 seconds. Add ice and shake for 12 seconds. Strain. Shake again for 8 seconds without ice. Double strain into a chilled Gimlet glass.

LEMON-INFUSED VODKA

Vodka .... 700ml | 24fl oz
Lemon segments (supremes) .... 200g | 7oz
Lemon zest .... 9g | ¼oz

Place all ingredients in an airtight container in the refrigerator for 24 hours. Strain and refrigerate until ready to use.

LEMON VERBENA SYRUP

Filtered water .... 120ml | 4fl oz
Superfine sugar .... 120g | 4oz
Lemon zest .... 7g | ¼oz
Dried lemon verbena .... 5g | 1tsp

Bring water to 100°C | 212°F. Pour over sugar, lemon zest, and verbena in a heatproof bowl. Stir until sugar dissolves. Infuse for 10 minutes. Filter and refrigerate until ready to use.

The tanginess of lemon is at the heart of this cocktail. In this recipe, I haven't focused on the acidity of the lemon, but rather on the indulgent richness that can be drawn from it – a sort of liquid lemon pie.

ISADORA

Tequila blanco .... 30ml | 1fl oz
Cherry Ratafia .... 30ml | 1fl oz
Verjus .... 2.5ml | ½tsp
Cherry liqueur .... 2.5ml | ½tsp

Combine all ingredients in a stainless steel mixing tin with ice. Stir for 20 seconds. Strain into a chilled Gimlet glass.

YELLOW

Fresh lemon juice .... 30ml | 1fl oz
Yellow Chartreuse .... 30ml | 1fl oz
Gentiane liqueur .... 25ml | ¾fl oz
London dry gin .... 20ml | ⅔fl oz
Lemon twist

Combine all ingredients in a shaker with ice. Hard shake for 4 seconds. Double strain into a coupette. Discard lemon twist.

Yellow is a cocktail that has been on the menu at Cravan since its opening in 2018 in Paris's 16th arrondissement.

For a long time, I wanted to explore bitterness while creating a perfectly balanced cocktail. During my research for the writing of *French Moderne*, I came across a 1920s recipe that was served with equal parts gin, Suze, and Yellow Chartreuse.

I reworked it, drawing inspiration from the structure of a Last Word, while keeping the focus on the bitterness brought by gentian. This is balanced by the roundness of the Yellow Chartreuse, all wrapped in the acidity of fresh lemon.

DAIQUIRI

Cuban rum .... 50ml | 1¾fl oz
Fresh lime juice .... 25ml | ¾fl oz
Simple syrup .... 15ml | ½fl oz

Combine all ingredients in a shaker with ice. Shake for 20 seconds. Double strain into a chilled coupette.

SIMPLE SYRUP See page 70.

WHISKEY SOUR

Bourbon	40ml | 1⅓fl oz
Egg white	25ml | ¾fl oz
Fresh lemon juice	20ml | ⅔fl oz
Simple syrup	15ml | ½fl oz
Angostura bitters	2 dashes

Place the bourbon, egg white, lemon juice, and simple syrup in a shaker without ice and shake for 12 seconds. Add ice and shake for 12 seconds. Double strain into a chilled Gimlet glass. Add 2 dashes of Angostura bitters on top.

SIMPLE SYRUP See page 70.

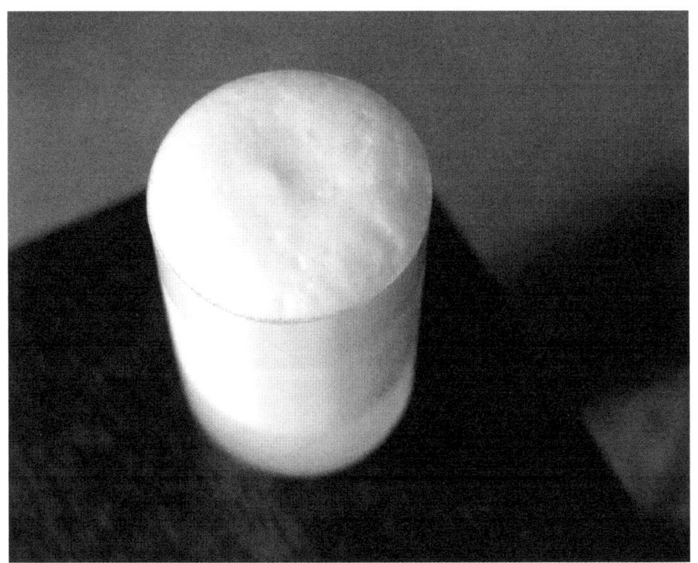

SILVER GIN FIZZ

London dry gin .... 40ml | 1⅓fl oz
Egg white .... 20ml | ⅔fl oz
Fresh lemon juice .... 20ml | ⅔fl oz
Simple syrup .... 20ml | ⅔fl oz
Orange blossom water .... 2 drops
Soda water .... top

Add the gin, egg white, lemon juice, syrup, and orange blossom water to a shaker without ice and dry shake for 8 seconds. Add ice and shake for 12 seconds. Strain out the ice, shake again for 8 seconds, then double strain into a highball glass. Top with soda water.

SIMPLE SYRUP See page 70.

PERFECT LADY

- White peach gin .... 40ml | 1⅓fl oz
- Egg white .... 25ml | ¾fl oz
- Fresh lemon juice .... 20ml | ⅔fl oz
- Simple syrup .... 15ml | ½fl oz
- Peychaud's bitters .... 1 dash

Place all ingredients in a shaker without ice and shake for 8 seconds. Add ice and shake for 12 seconds. Strain out the ice and shake again for 8 seconds. Double strain into a Nick & Nora glass.

WHITE PEACH GIN

- White peaches .... 300g | 11oz
- London dry gin .... 700ml | 24floz

Peel, pit, and quarter the peaches. Combine with gin in an airtight container and refrigerate for 48 hours. Strain and store in the refrigerator.

SIMPLE SYRUP See page 70.

NO COMMENT

- Bitter orange vodka .... 35ml | 1¼fl oz
- Bitter orange cordial .... 30ml | 1fl oz
- Simple syrup .... 25ml | ¾fl oz
- Bitter orange twist

Add all ingredients to a stainless steel mixing tin with ice and stir for 35 seconds. Double strain into a coupe. Discard bitter orange twist.

BITTER ORANGE VODKA

- Vodka .... 700g | 24fl oz
- Bitter orange segments (supremes) 200g | 7oz
- Bitter orange zest .... 9g | ⅓oz

Place all ingredients in an airtight container and refrigerate for 24 hours. Strain and refrigerate.

BITTER ORANGE CORDIAL

- Water .... 500ml | 17fl oz
- Bitter orange juice .... 250ml | 8fl oz
- Superfine sugar .... 200g | 7oz
- Bitter orange zest .... 4g | 1tsp
- Tartaric acid .... 2g | ½tsp

Bring water to 100°C | 212°F. Pour over juice, sugar, zest, and acid in a heatproof bowl. Stir until sugar and acid are fully dissolved. Infuse for 24 hours. Strain and refrigerate.

SIMPLE SYRUP See page 70.

C+

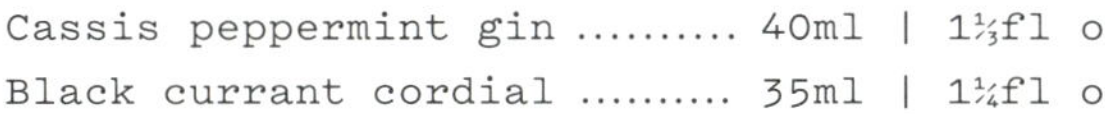

Cassis peppermint gin .... 40ml | 1⅓fl oz
Black currant cordial .... 35ml | 1¼fl oz

Add ingredients to a stainless steel mixing tin with ice and stir for 15 seconds. Double strain into a chilled Gimlet glass.

CASSIS PEPPERMINT GIN

London dry gin .... 700ml | 24fl oz
Fresh black currants .... 250g | 9oz
Dried peppermint .... 1g | ¼tsp

Place ingredients in an airtight container and refrigerate for 24 hours. Filter through a pre-moistened paper filter. Store refrigerated.

BLACK CURRANT CORDIAL

Filtered water .... 500ml | 17fl oz
Organic black currant juice 250ml | 8fl oz
Superfine sugar .... 200g | 7oz
Tartaric acid .... 2.5g | ½tsp

Bring water to 100°C | 212°F. Pour over the juice and sugar in a heatproof bowl. Add the acid and stir until sugar and acid are fully dissolved. Store refrigerated.

Two cocktails celebrating black currant. The first version (C+) captures a refreshing liveliness, with peppermint adding a crisp, bright note. The second one (C++) delves deeper into the essence of black currant, highlighting its rich, layered flavors and natural depth.

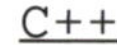

C++

Black currant-leaf-infused
cognac .... 30ml | 1fl oz
Black currant cordial .... 25ml | ¾fl oz
Black currant liqueur .... 5ml | 1tsp

Add all ingredients to a mixing stainless steel tin with ice and stir for 12 seconds. Double strain into a chilled Gimlet glass.

BLACK CURRANT-LEAF-INFUSED COGNAC

Dried black currant leaves .... 2g | ½tsp
Cognac VS .... 100ml | 3½fl oz
Black currant pepper tincture .... 1 dash

Vacuum-seal the cognac and black currant leaves in a vacuum-seal bag and cook sous-vide at 60°C | 140°F for 30 minutes. Stop the cooking by plunging the bag into an ice bath. Filter through a premoistened paper filter. Add the tincture and stir. Refrigerate until ready to use.

BLACK CURRANT PEPPER TINCTURE

96% neutral alcohol .... 10ml | ⅓fl oz
Black currant pepper .... 3g | 1tsp

Vacuum-seal the alcohol and pepper in a vacuum-seal bag and cook sous-vide at 60°C | 140°F for 1 hour. Stop the cooking by plunging the bag into an ice bath. Filter through a premoistened paper filter.

BLACK CURRANT CORDIAL

Organic black currant juice 100ml | 3½fl oz
Filtered water .... 15ml | ½fl oz
Superfine sugar .... 15g | ½oz
Malic acid .... 0.5g | ⅛tsp

Pour the filtered water over juice and sugar in a heatproof bowl. Add the acid and stir until sugar and acid are fully dissolved. Store refrigerated.

CHERCHE MIDI

Cognac VS .... 40ml | 1⅓fl oz
Cider cordial .... 20ml | ⅔fl oz

Stir cognac and cordial with ice in a stainless steel mixing tin for 12 seconds. Double strain into a coupe.

CIDER CORDIAL

Cider .... 750ml | 25fl oz
Superfine sugar .... 250g | 9oz
Tartaric acid .... 1g | ¼tsp

Bring the cider to a boil. Once boiling, reduce the heat to a simmer and simmer for 5 minutes until slightly reduced. Add sugar and tartaric acid and stir until fully dissolved. Refrigerate until ready to use.

48°51' NORTH 2°19' EAST

Pineapple rum .... 40ml | 1⅓fl oz
Lime cordial .... 20ml | ⅔fl oz
Velvet falernum .... 2.5ml | ½tsp

Add all ingredients to a stainless steel mixing tin with ice and stir for 35 seconds. Double strain into a chilled Old-Fashioned glass.

PINEAPPLE RUM

Fresh pineapple peeled .... 300g | 11oz
7-year-old rum .... 700ml | 24fl oz

Cut the pineapple into 2 cm | ¾-inch cubes. Vacuum-seal half of the rum with the pineapple in a vacuum-seal bag. Refrigerate for 48 hours. Filter through a Superbag, then stir in the second half of the rum. Store in refrigerator.

LIME CORDIAL

Lime zest .... 5g | 1¾tsp
Lime juice .... 250ml | 8fl oz
Superfine sugar .... 200g | 7oz
Filtered water .... 500ml | 17fl oz
Tartaric acid .... 2.5g | 1tsp

In a heatproof pitcher, combine zest and juice with sugar. Bring the water to 90°C | 194°F then pour over the mixture. Add the acid. Stir until the sugar and acid have fully dissolved. Cover with plastic wrap and let infuse at room temperature for 24 hours. Strain and refrigerate.

STRAWBERRY & RHUBARB

Strawberry-infused vodka ..... 40ml | 1⅓fl oz
Rhubarb cordial .... 20ml | ⅔fl oz

Stir in a stainless steel mixing tin with ice for 15 seconds. Strain into a chilled aperitif glass.

STRAWBERRY-INFUSED VODKA

Strawberries (Anaïs variety) ..... 250g | 9oz
Vodka .... 700ml | 24fl oz
Simple syrup .... 10ml | 2tsp

Wash, hull, and halve the strawberries. Place in a vacuum-seal bag with vodka. Vacuum-seal and cook sous-vide at 52°C | 125.6°F for 1 hour. Strain through a sieve. Refrigerate until ready to use.

SIMPLE SYRUP See page 70.

RHUBARB CORDIAL

Rhubarb juice .... 250ml | 8fl oz
Superfine sugar .... 100g | 3½oz
Tartaric acid .... 0.5g | ⅛tsp

Press rhubarb with a cold-press juicer (you should have 250ml | 8fl oz). Filter through a Superbag. Dissolve sugar in the filtered rhubarb juice. Add acid and stir until sugar and acid are fully dissolved.

THE LADY FROM SHANGHAI

White peach gin .... 40ml | 1⅓fl oz
Lime cordial .... 20ml | ⅔fl oz
Jasmine tea syrup .... 10ml | ⅓fl oz

Stir all ingredients in a stainless steel mixing tin with ice for 14 seconds. Double strain into a chilled Gimlet glass.

WHITE PEACH GIN

White peaches .... 300g | 11oz
London dry gin .... 700ml | 24fl oz

Peel, pit, and quarter the peaches. Combine peaches and gin in an airtight container and refrigerate for 48 hours. Filter and refrigerate.

LIME CORDIAL See page 120.

JASMINE TEA SYRUP

Filtered water .... 120ml | 4fl oz
Superfine sugar .... 25g | 1oz
White jasmine tea .... 2g | 1tsp

Bring water to 100°C | 212°F. Pour over the sugar and tea in a heatproof bowl. Stir until sugar is fully dissolved. Infuse for 10 minutes. Strain and store refrigerated.

A COUNTESS FROM HONG KONG

Mandarin cordial .... 30ml | 1fl oz
Earl Grey vodka .... 30ml | 1fl oz

Stir ingredients in a stainless steel mixing tin with ice for 20 seconds. Double strain into a Gimlet glass.

MANDARIN CORDIAL

Filtered water .... 600ml | 20fl oz
Mandarin juice .... 250ml | 8fl oz
Mandarin zest .... 10g | 1tbsp
Superfine sugar .... 200g | 7oz
Tartaric acid .... 2.5g | 1tsp

Bring water to 100°C | 212°F. Pour over the zest, juice, sugar, and acid in a heatproof bowl. Stir until the sugar and acid dissolve. Let infuse at room temperature for 24 hours. Strain and refrigerate.

EARL GREY VODKA

Vodka .... 350ml | 12fl oz
Earl Grey tea .... 5g | 1¾tsp

Infuse the vodka and tea at room temperature for 10 minutes. Strain and refrigerate.

KA

5-citrus jam cordial .... 40ml | 1⅓fl oz
Yuzu green tea vodka .... 30ml | 1fl oz
Sparkling sake .... 25ml | ¾fl oz

Stir the cordial and vodka in a stainless steel mixing tin with ice for 8 seconds. Double strain into a chilled Gimlet glass. Top with the sparkling sake.

5-CITRUS JAM CORDIAL

Filtered water .... 175ml | 6fl oz
5-citrus jam or marmalade .... 30g | 5tsp

Place the water and jam in a vacuum-seal bag. Vacuum-seal and cook sous-vide at 60°C | 140°F for 30 minutes. Plunge the bag into ice to stop the cooking. Filter through a coffee filter when fully cooled. Store in refrigerator.

YUZU GREEN TEA VODKA

Vodka .... 200ml | 7fl oz
Yuzu green tea .... 3g | 1tsp

Infuse the vodka and tea at room temperature for 10 minutes. Filter through a coffee filter. Store in refrigerator.

MOTO

Cognac VS .... 30ml | 1fl oz
Fermented tea syrup .... 25ml | ¾fl oz
Traditional sake.................... 20ml | ⅔fl oz

Stir ingredients in a stainless steel mixing tin with ice for 15 seconds. Double strain into a chilled Gimlet glass.

FERMENTED TEA SYRUP

Filtered water .... 120ml | 4fl oz
Superfine sugar .... 20g | 1oz
Fermented tea .... 2g | 1tsp

Pour (boiling 100°C | 212°F) water over the sugar and tea in a heatproof bowl. Stir until the sugar dissolves. Infuse for 10 minutes. Filter and store in refrigerator.

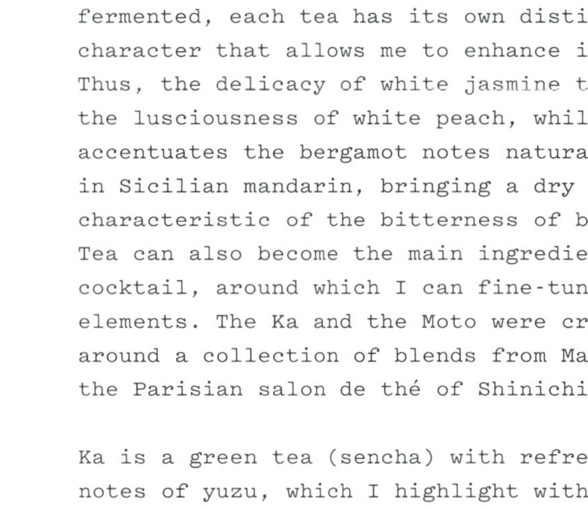

Whether green, white, or black, smoked or fermented, each tea has its own distinct character that allows me to enhance ingredients. Thus, the delicacy of white jasmine tea reveals the lusciousness of white peach, while Earl Grey accentuates the bergamot notes naturally present in Sicilian mandarin, bringing a dry finish characteristic of the bitterness of black tea. Tea can also become the main ingredient of a cocktail, around which I can fine-tune certain elements. The Ka and the Moto were created around a collection of blends from Maison Ogata, the Parisian salon de thé of Shinichiro Ogata.

Ka is a green tea (sencha) with refreshing notes of yuzu, which I highlight with a citrus marmalade. Moto, on the other hand - a fermented tea undergoing lactic fermentation - pairs perfectly with Cognac, to which we add a sake, expressing chocolate notes.

ESPRESSO MARTINI

Cold brew coffee .... 50ml | 1¾fl oz
Vodka .... 25ml | ¾fl oz
Simple syrup .... 5ml | 1tsp
Coffee liqueur .... 2.5ml | ½tsp

Add all ingredients to a shaker with ice and shake for 5 seconds. Strain out the ice and shake again briefly. Double strain into a chilled Gimlet glass.

COLD BREW COFFEE

Coffee beans .... 50g | 2oz or ¼cup
Filtered water .... 200ml | 7fl oz

Grind beans medium-fine. Combine the ground coffee and water in an airtight container and refrigerate for 24 hours. Filter through a bouillon strainer and let rest for 30 minutes. Filter again. Store in refrigerator.

SIMPLE SYRUP See page 70.

EXPRESS MARTINI

Vodka .... 25ml | ¾fl oz
Espresso .... 25ml | ¾fl oz
Simple syrup .... 10ml | ⅓fl oz

Hard shake all ingredients with ice for 5 seconds. Double strain into a small shot glass.

SIMPLE SYRUP See page 70.

NOT AN ESPRESSO MARTINI

Dried-coffee-leaf-infused
vodka .... 30ml | 1fl oz
Cascara coffee cordial .... 30ml | 1fl oz
Coffee tincture .... 1 drop

Add vodka and cordial to a stainless steel mixing tin filled with ice and stir for 17 seconds. Add the tincture. Double strain into a chilled coupe glass.

COFFEE-LEAF-INFUSED VODKA

Vodka .... 100ml | 3½fl oz
Cognac VS .... 2.5ml | ½tsp
Dried coffee leaves .... 2g | 1tsp

Roughly crumble the coffee leaves and combine with vodka and cognac in a vacuum-seal bag. Vacuum-seal and cook sous-vide at 52°C | 125.6°F for 20 minutes. Cool, strain, and refrigerate.

CASCARA COFFEE CORDIAL

Ethiopian cascara coffee .... 15g | ½oz
Filtered water .... 100ml | 3½fl oz
Superfine sugar .... 15g | ½oz
Tartaric acid .... 1 pinch

Infuse cascara in water in an airtight container and refrigerate for 24 hours. Strain, add sugar and acid, and stir until sugar and acid are fully dissolved. Refrigerate.

COFFEE TINCTURE

Ethiopian coffee beans .... 4g | 1tsp
96% neutral alcohol .... 10ml | ⅓fl oz

Grind beans medium-fine and place in a vacuum-sealed bag with neutral alcohol. Vacuum-seal and cook sous-vide at 60°C | 140°F for 1 hour. Plunge the bag in ice water to stop the cooking. Filter through a coffee filter once fully cooled.

OLD FASHIONED

Bourbon .... 50ml | 1¾fl oz
Simple syrup .... 10ml | ⅓fl oz
Angostura bitters .... 3 dashes
Orange zest

Add bourbon, simple syrup, and bitters to a mixing glass. Add ice and stir for 20 seconds. Double strain into a glass with ice. Garnish with a long twist of orange zest.

SIMPLE SYRUP See page 70.

SAZERAC

Absinthe .... 5ml | 1tsp
Simple syrup .... 5ml | 1tsp
Cognac VSOP .... 50ml | 1¾fl oz
Peychaud's bitters .... 3 dashes
Lemon twist

Add absinthe and 2 ice cubes to a glass and stir for 5 seconds. In a stainless steel mixing tin with ice, stir the remaining ingredients for 12 seconds. Discard the absinthe from the glass and double strain the mixture into it. Discard lemon twist.

SIMPLE SYRUP See page 70.

BOBBY BURNS

Sweet vermouth .... 30ml | 1fl oz
Peated whisky .... 30ml | 1fl oz
Benedictine DOM .... 10ml | ⅓fl oz

Add all ingredients to a stainless steel mixing tin with ice and stir for 12 seconds. Double strain into a Gimlet glass.

REMEMBER THE MAINE

Cherry liqueur .... 2.5ml | ½tsp
Sweet vermouth .... 25ml | ¾fl oz
Rye whiskey .... 30ml | 1fl oz
Absinthe .... 3 dashes
Kirsch cherry

Add all ingredients to a stainless steel mixing tin with ice and stir for 20 seconds. Double strain into a coupe glass. Garnish with a kirsch cherry.

CHAMPAGNE COCKTAIL

Champagne reduction .... 50ml | 1¾fl oz
Cognac VSOP .... 25ml | ¾fl oz
Angostura bitters reduction ...... 2.5ml | ½tsp

Add all ingredients to a stainless steel mixing tin with ice and stir for 10 seconds. Double strain into a coupe glass.

CHAMPAGNE REDUCTION

Champagne brut .... 500ml | 17fl oz
Superfine sugar .... 75g | 2½oz

Pour the Champagne into a saucepan and set over medium heat. Bring to a boil. Once boiling, reduce heat and bring to a simmer. Continue simmering for 10 minutes. Add sugar and stir until completely dissolved. Cover with plastic wrap and let cool. Store in refrigerator.

ANGOSTURA REDUCTION

Angostura bitters .... 200ml | 7fl oz

Pour the Angostura into a saucepan and set over high heat. Bring to a boil. Once boiling, reduce heat and bring to a simmer. Continue simmering for 10 minutes. The bitters should be reduced by half. Filter through a coffee filter and let cool. Store in refrigerator.

MM

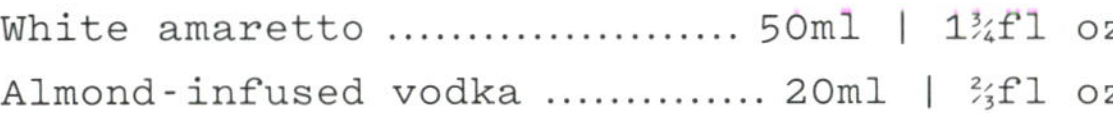

White amaretto .... 50ml | 1¾fl oz
Almond-infused vodka .... 20ml | ⅔fl oz

Add ingredients to a stainless steel mixing tin with ice and stir for 30 seconds. Double strain into a chilled coupe glass.

ALMOND-INFUSED VODKA

Almonds .... 200g | 7oz
Vodka .... 700ml | 24fl oz

Crush the almonds with a chopper. Weigh separately, then combine the almonds and vodka in a vacuum-sealed bag. Refrigerate for 5 days. Filter the vodka using a Superbag. Store in refrigerator.

XMAS EDITION

- Cognac VS .... 30ml | 1fl oz
- Benedictine DOM .... 15ml | ½fl oz
- Amaro .... 5ml | 1tsp
- Angostura bitters .... 1 dash

Add all ingredients to a stainless steel mixing tin with ice and stir for 12 seconds. Strain into a coupe glass.

Taste the balance

The technique of collage consists in taking a certain number of elements from already existing works, objects, or messages, and integrating them into a new creation in order to produce an original whole in which various kinds of ruptures appear.

Such a formulation, necessarily imprecise because deliberately very general, has at least the advantage of highlighting the four essential characteristics of collage in the strict sense:
(1) a cutting-out, (2) of pre-formed messages, (3) followed by an assemblage, (4) with internal ruptures.

In summary: a selection and a combination, like any other message, but with the double constitutive condition of borrowing from already organized sets and arranging them into a system of allotropes.

In *Collages, Revue d'esthétique*,
no. 3-4/1978
Union Générale d'Éditions, 1978

Collage

RAVAN

Details

QUAD 405

BANG & OLUFSEN

The world of cocktails sometimes seems swept away by its own frenzy. Initially fruitful, this wave has at times carried away with it any sense of restraint. Just as I have sought in the history of the craft a framework for our creations, I always return to simplicity when imagining our offerings.

Our cocktails strive to be simple and precise, without ever forgetting to remain complex. We limit the number of ingredients in each cocktail, which forces us to pay close attention to pairings and measurements in a pursuit of precision. To me, this seems absolutely essential in maintaining a clear direction and ensuring great consistency. Week after week, a Yellow will always display that same bitter character, just as the Luco will consistently reveal its vegetal notes.

That is the core of our creative challenge: to succeed in presenting the most balanced and refined creation, without renouncing either its complexity or its expressiveness.

This deliberate simplicity, to me, is truly synonymous with exception – an exception that defies the rule, for it is in the nature of rules to seek the death of exceptions.

We refuse to standardize our creations. An obsession with the smallest detail. A devotion to precision that is reflected both in the choice of glassware, since its shape, its weight, play a decisive role in the appreciation of a cocktail, and in a particular attachment to a sense of purity, for we always keep in mind that a silhouette stripped of its ornaments must fall perfectly into place.

E

Exception

I approach our bar food at Cravan the same way I do our cocktails: I look for simplicity and clear, striking flavors that stand out for their originality. That's why I put together distinctive or classic dishes using just a few ingredients.

Food

GILDA

Recipe for 1 piece

Guindilla .... 1 piece
Anchovy fillet in oil .... 1 piece
Olives .... 2 pieces

Skewer the ingredients on a wooden pick: olive, anchovy, olive, guindilla.

Drizzle with a dash of olive oil.

The Gilda is a classic pintxo from the Basque Country. Created in San Sebastián, it has become one of the most famous thanks to its disarming simplicity and perfectly balanced flavors.

Olive, anchovy, and guindilla (a small Basque sweet chili pickled in vinegar) combine in a perfect bite for an aperitif.

DEVILED EGGS WITH BONITO

Recipe for 12 pieces

6 EGGS

MAYONNAISE

Egg yolk .... 1 piece
Mustard .... 15g | ½oz
Bonito vinegar .... 15ml | ½fl oz
Bonito flakes (*katsuobushi*)

Make a mayonnaise with the egg yolk, mustard, and vinegar, whisking in a glass of neutral oil. Boil the 6 eggs for 10 minutes, then peel and cut them in half. Remove the yolks and mix them with the mayonnaise. Fill the whites with the yolk mixture.
Plate and sprinkle generously with bonito flakes.

I am a great admirer of *katsuobushi*, this preparation of dried, fermented, and smoked bonito in flakes, also used for dashi.

Japanese rice vinegars – whether bonito, citrus, or plum – are another source of inspiration. Here, the classic deviled eggs take on smoky notes and end with that mysterious umami touch.

VEGETABLE PISSALADIÈRE

Recipe for 10 pieces

FLAKY PASTRY DOUGH

ONION COMPOTE

Yellow onions .... 1kg | 2¼lb

Butter .... 100g | 3½oz

Thyme, bay leaf, rosemary

Peel and slice the onions thinly. Cook slowly with butter, thyme, rosemary, and bay leaf until soft and sweet.

VEGETARIAN TAPENADE

Raw red beets .... 300g | 11oz

Pitted black olives .... 200g | 7oz

Pickled capers .... 50g | 1¾oz

Roast beets on a bed of coarse salt at 170°C (340°F) for 1.5 hours. Peel and cut into 4 cm (1½ inch) chunks. Vacuum-seal with 2% salt by weight and ferment 3-7 days at room temperature (below 26°C (78.8°F)). Blend beets, olives, and capers roughly.

Preheat oven to 180°C (355°F). Roll the puff pastry to 1 cm (½ inch) thick and cut into 11 cm (4⅓ inch) circles. Top with onion compote, leaving a 1 cm (½ inch) border. Bake for 17 minutes. When serving, add tapenade, cut into quarters, and finish with chopped chives, cracked pepper, and a drizzle of olive oil.

Here we've reimagined the Niçoise classic, replacing the anchovy paste with fermented beetroot, creating a plant-based tapenade where the fermentation beautifully enhances the flavor.

SCALLOPS WITH ARDBERG WHISKY

Recipe for 6 pieces

6 SCALLOPS

BEURRE BLANC

Ardbeg Scotch Whisky .... 50ml | 1¾fl oz
Heavy cream .... 200ml | 7fl oz
Butter .... 50g | 1¾oz
Shallots .... 4 pieces
Fleur de sel

Finely chop and sweat the shallots. Add the whisky and reduce to dry without browning.
Add cream and reduce until slightly thickened, then whisk in cold butter.
At serving time, sear the scallops presentation-side down. Warm the beurre blanc and pour it over the scallops on the plate, finishing with a touch of fleur de sel.

On the Isle of Islay, it's common to taste freshly caught raw scallops on the harbor with a splash of Ardbeg whisky. I drew inspiration from this custom to reinterpret the classic French beurre blanc, replacing white wine with whisky.

ONSEN TAMAGO

Recipe for 6 servings

6 EGGS

DASHI BROTH

Water .... 1.5l | 50fl oz
Kombu .... 15g | ½oz
Bonito flakes (*katsuobushi*) .... 10g | ⅓oz
Soy sauce .... 160ml | 5½fl oz
Mirin .... 160ml | 5½fl oz

Soak the kombu in water for 24 hours.
Combine mirin, soy sauce, and bonito flakes, and simmer gently for 15 minutes. Heat the filtered kombu water and reduce to 1 liter, then strain again. Filter the soy-mirin-bonito broth and combine the two preparations. Let cool.
Cook the eggs for 1 hour at 63°C (145°F) using a sous-vide or steam oven. Peel an egg and place it in a bowl, half-covered with dashi broth. Garnish with chopped scallions.

Broths, much like cocktails, are full of surprises. *Onsen tamago* (lit. hot spring egg) perfectly illustrates this solid-liquid harmony.

PARIS MUSHROOMS, BLACK TRUFFLE

Recipe for 1 plate

Large white button mushrooms .... 3 pieces
Black truffle .... 1 piece
Egg yolks .... 2 pieces
Fleur de sel and pepper

Cut the mushrooms in half and slice thinly on a mandolin. Arrange on a plate.
Lightly beat the two egg yolks in a glass and pour over the mushrooms.
Season with fleur de sel and pepper.
Grate the black truffle over the top using a microplane.

It's good to remember that egg yolk is a condiment that saves many situations.

Here is a raw mushroom-on-mushroom pairing where the yolk brings luscious richness.

MASHED POTATOES WITH CAVIAR

Recipe for 5 servings

CAVIAR

POTATO PURÉE

Mona Lisa potatoes (large size) .... 1kg | 2¼lb
Milk .... 200ml | 7fl oz
Cream .... 100ml | 3½fl oz
Butter .... 250g | 9oz

Heat the milk and cream with one-third of the butter. Bake the potatoes whole on a bed of coarse salt at 190°C (375°F) until tender. Scoop out the flesh. Pass through a sieve.

Over heat, blend with the warm milk-cream-butter mixture, gradually incorporating the remaining cold butter until smooth and silky.
Serve hot in a bowl topped with two generous quenelles of caviar.

The rusticity of the potato combined with the smooth luxury of caviar is a modern classic.

Our choice was to marry creaminess with creaminess, inspired by Joël Robuchon's legendary purée.

VEAL CARPACCIO WITH TONNATO SAUCE

Recipe for 1 plate

VEAL

Noix de veau .... 100g | 3½oz

TONNATO SAUCE

Egg yolk .... 1 piece
Sherry vinegar .... 15ml | ½fl oz
Mustard .... 30g | 1oz
Capers .... 15g | ½oz
Anchovy fillets .... 15g | ½oz
Lemon juice .... 5ml | 1tsp
Neutral oil .... 25ml | ¾fl oz
Canned tuna .... 250g | 9oz
Fleur de sel and pepper

Combine egg yolk, sherry vinegar, and mustard in a bowl and rest 2 minutes. Add 4-5 turns of pepper.

Whisk in oil to make a mayonnaise.
Blend with capers, anchovies, lemon juice, and tuna until smooth.

Slice the veal thinly (not too fine), arrange on a plate, season, and top with 3 spoonfuls of tonnato sauce and a few caper berries.

Vitello tonnato appears on many bar menus, but I've always found the sauce overwhelms the meat. Here, the veal (Aubrac veal, served raw as carpaccio) takes center stage, with the sauce playing a supporting role.

RAZOR CLAMS WITH SALSA VERDE

Recipe for 1 plate

5 RAZOR CLAMS

SALSA VERDE

Capers .... 30g | 1oz
Anchovies .... 30g | 1oz
Parsley .... 2 bunches
Olive oil

Blend all ingredients, emulsifying with olive oil until it reaches pesto consistency.
Sear the razor clams quickly in a hot pan with a drizzle of oil.

Plate and spoon over plenty of salsa verde.

The meaty, briny clams pair beautifully with the herbaceous freshness of parsley and olive oil.

ETON MESS

Recipe for 10 servings

FRENCH MERINGUE

Ingredient	Metric	Imperial
Sugar	20g	¾oz
Icing sugar	40g	1½oz
Egg whites	60g	2oz

Whip the egg whites with granulated sugar, then fold in icing sugar until soft peaks form. Pipe and dry in the oven at 70°C (160°F) for 2 hours until crisp.

FONTAINEBLEAU

Ingredient	Metric	Imperial
Full-fat fromage blanc	200g	7oz
Heavy cream	200ml	7fl oz

Whip fromage blanc and cream together until airy.

FRUIT COULIS

Ingredient	Metric	Imperial
Water	20ml	⅔fl oz
Sugar	20g	¾oz
Fruit (adjust sugar and sweetness)	200g	7oz

Make a simple syrup, add fruit, simmer, and blend.

FRUIT SYRUP

Ingredient	Metric	Imperial
Water	300ml	10fl oz
Sugar	30g	1oz
Fruit	200g	7oz

Make a 30% sugar syrup, bring to a boil, add fruit, and cool.
To serve: place spoonfuls of Fontainebleau on a plate, add broken meringue pieces, top with fruit and syrup.

A classic I simply adore. Try a winter version inspired by Mont-Blanc with chestnuts instead of fruit. Remember - the plate should look deliciously messy!

Not Fancy

G

Garnish

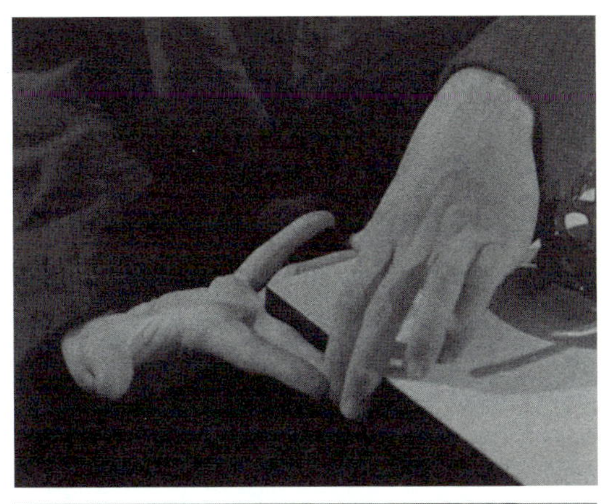
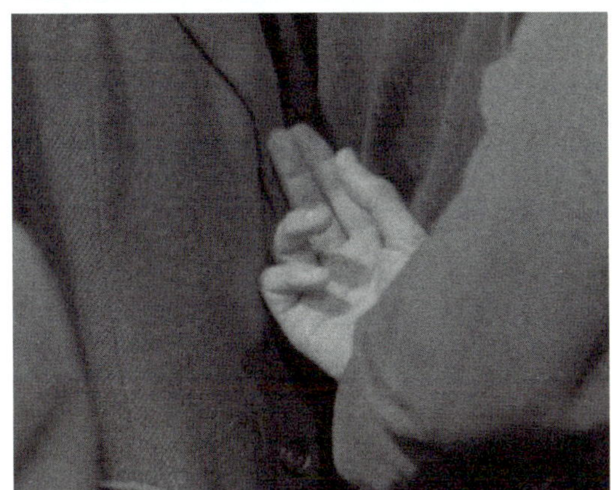
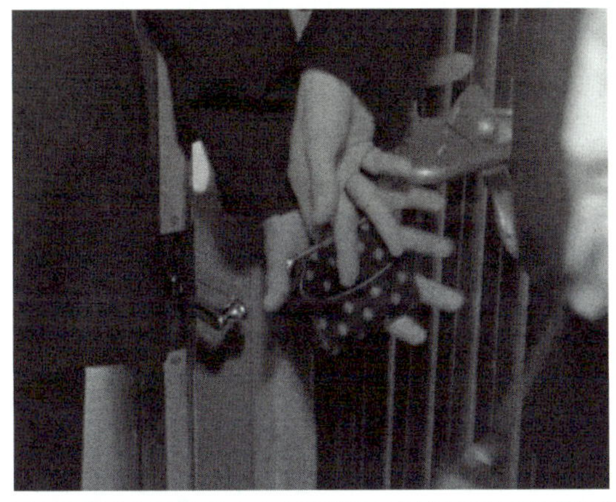
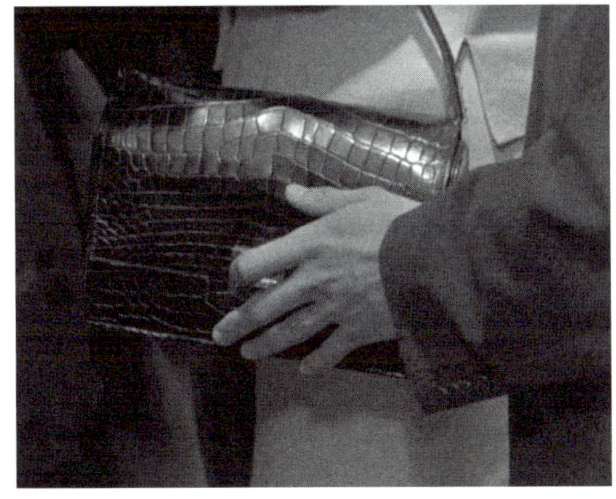

Hand

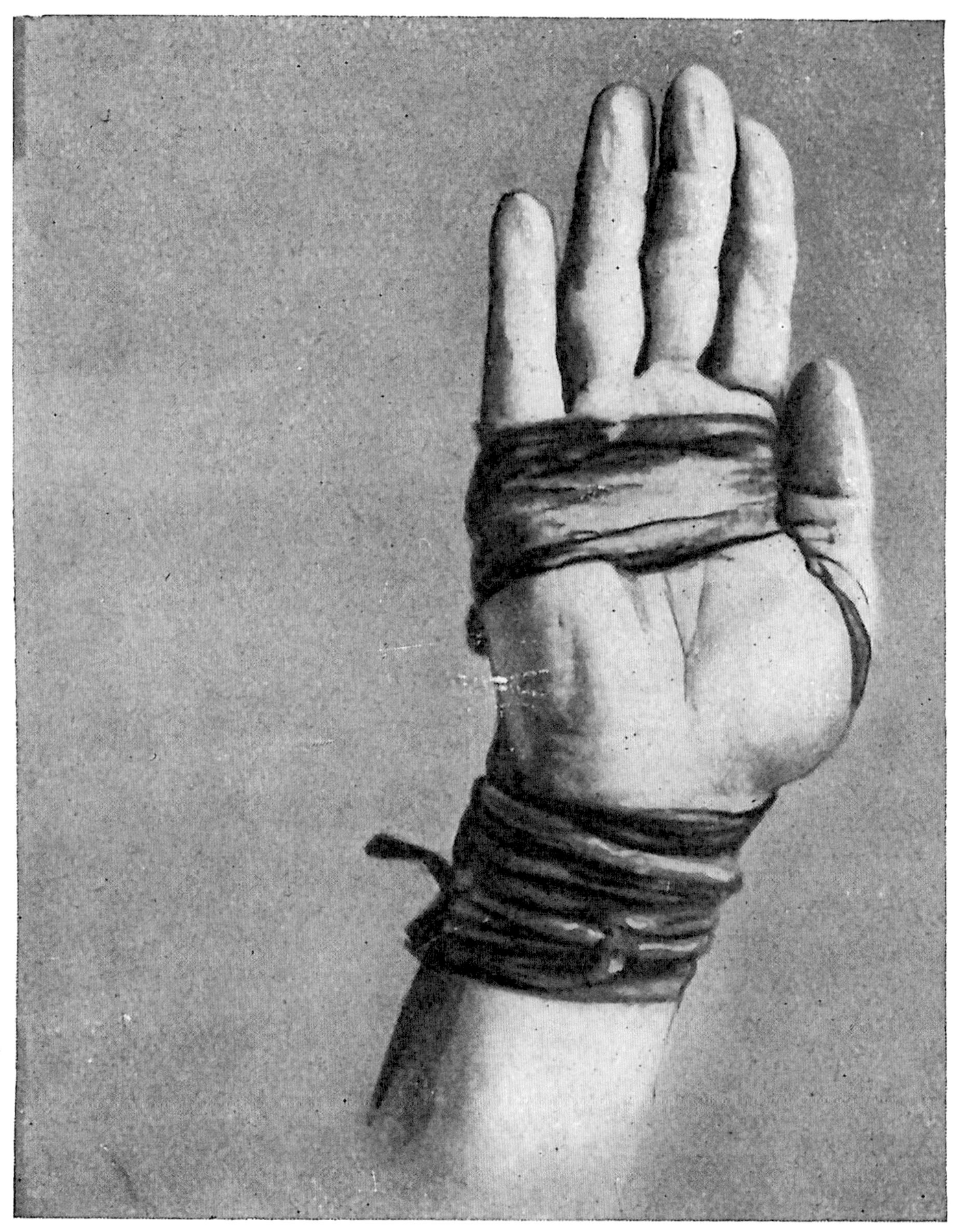

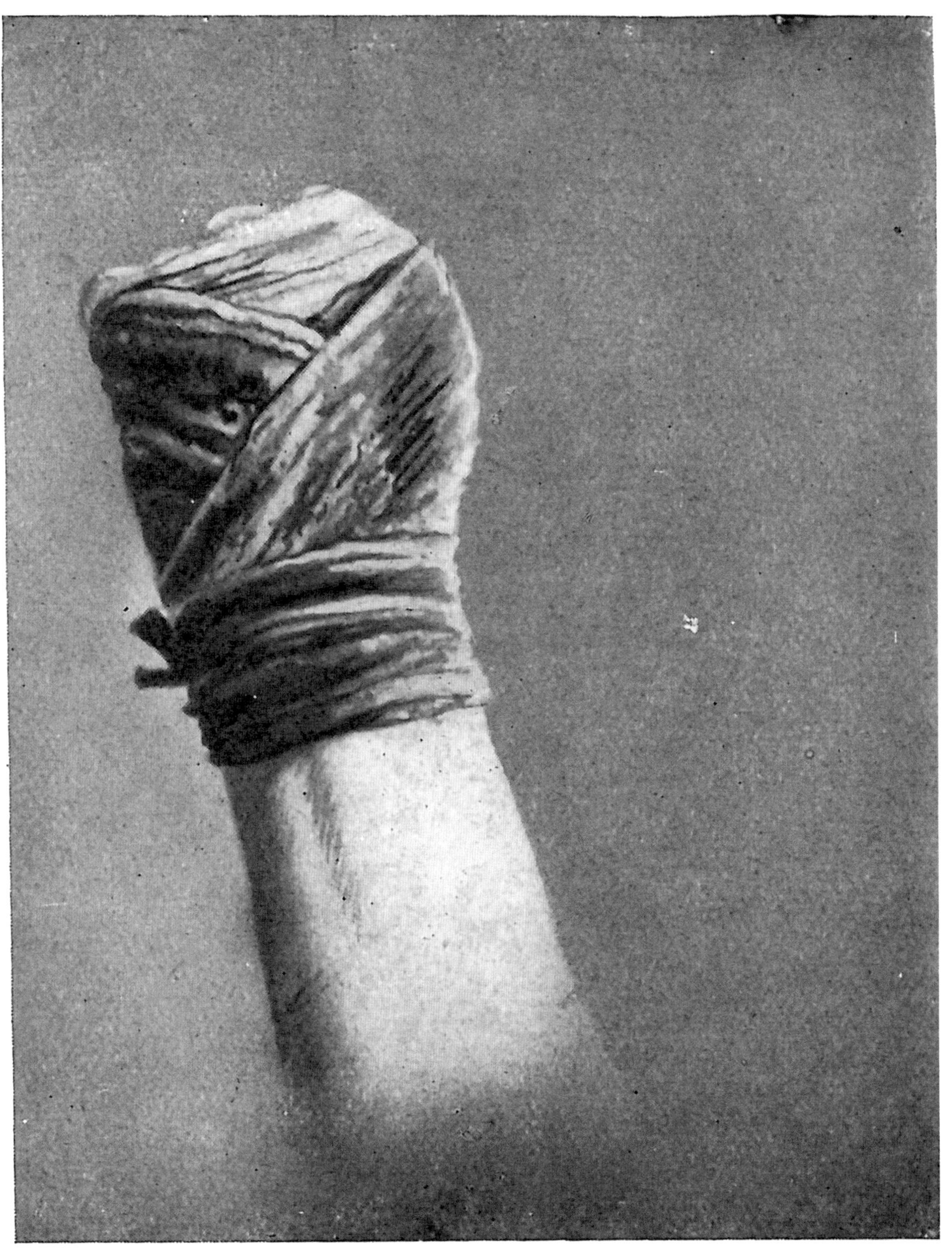

12.
Séparation infra-mince entre
le bruit de detonation d'un fusil
(très proche) et
l'apparition de la marque de
la balle sur la cible ——————
(distance maximum 1 à 4 metres.
- Tir de foire)

12.
Infra-mince separation between
the sound of the detonation of a gun
(very close) and the
appearance of the mark of
the bullet on the target ——————
(maximum distance 1 to 4 meters.
- Shooting range at a fair)

Marcel Duchamp
Notes Infra-mince, 1930
Translated by Rebecca Loewen,

Infra-mince / The In-Between

We too often confuse luxury and wealth for elegance. […] A well-dressed person will always outshine one merely arrayed in their riches.

Though no longer marked by clear distinctions, clothing still carries subtle nuances, faint lines of demarcation that betray to the trained eye one's age, fortune, and profession. The tailors of Paris know how to capture and preserve these imperceptible differences with rare skill. The lawyer, the landowner, the doctor, the investor, and the dandy – though dressed by the same tailor, with the same piece of cloth, cut from the same patterns – each wear a different suit.

Horace Raisson, 1840
In Emilie Hammen, *The Idea of Fashion. A New History, Vol. 1*
Éditions B42, 2023

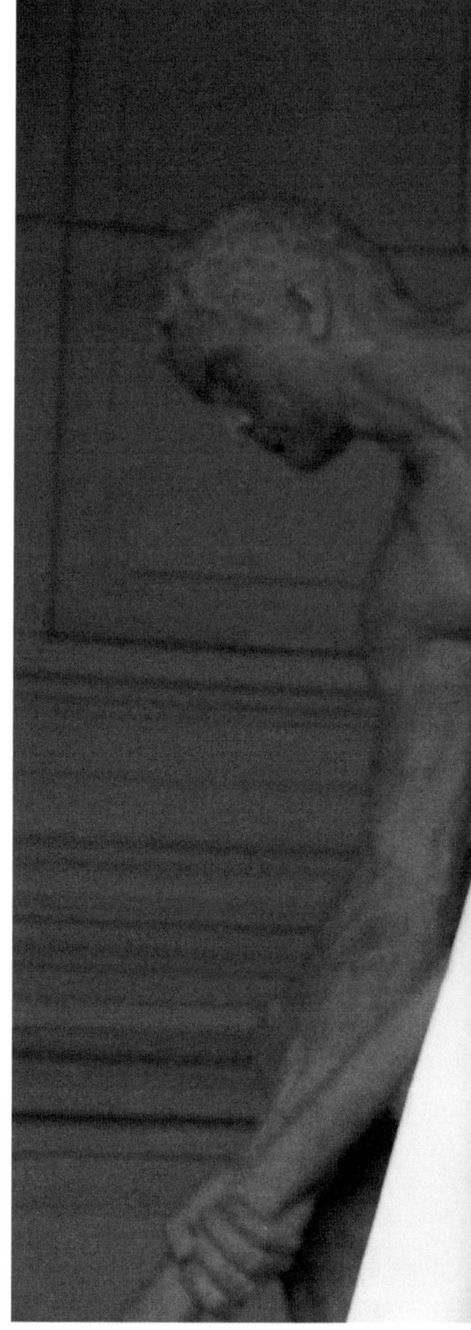

J

Jacket

JACK JOHNSON=ARTHUR CRAVAN

K

Knockout

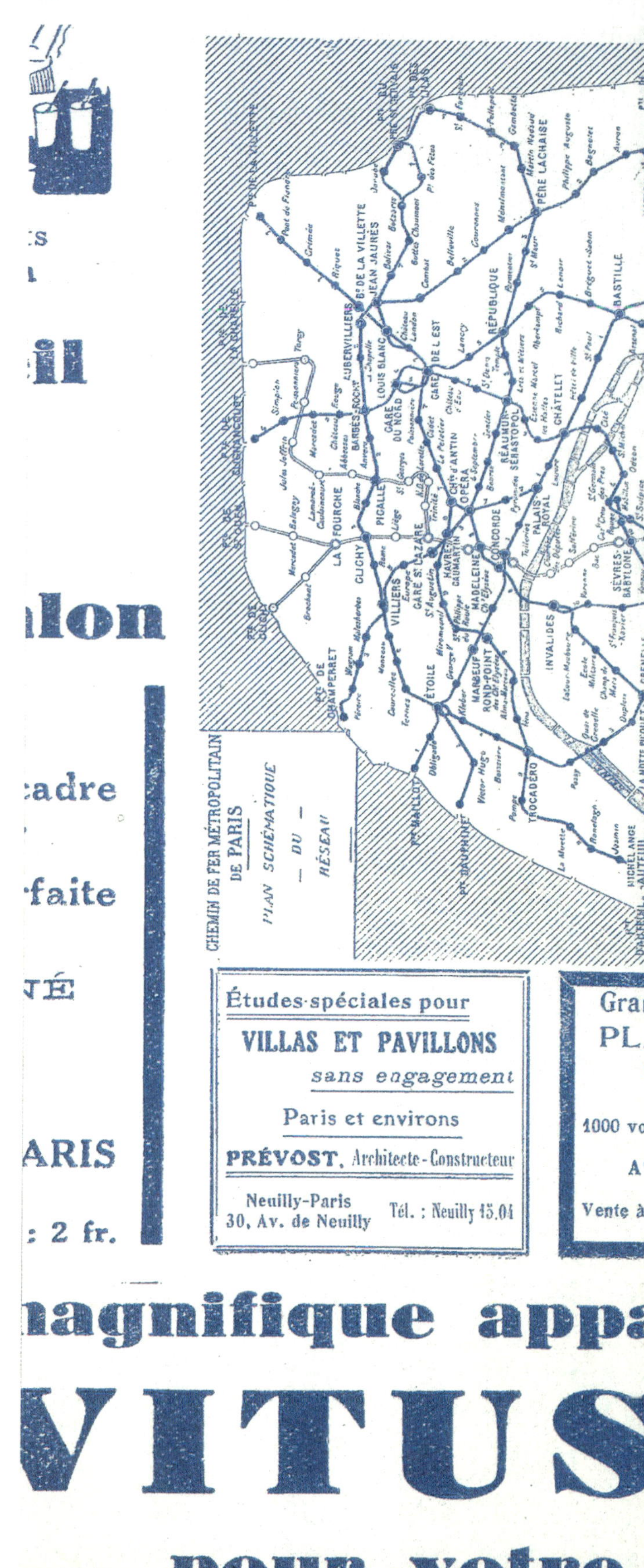

:il

alon

cadre

rfaite

NÉ

ARIS

: 2 fr.

CHEMIN DE FER MÉTROPOLITAIN DE PARIS

— PLAN SCHÉMATIQUE — DU — RÉSEAU

Études spéciales pour

VILLAS ET PAVILLONS

sans engagement

Paris et environs

PRÉVOST, Architecte-Constructeur

Neuilly-Paris
30, Av. de Neuilly

Tél. : Neuilly 15.04

Gran

PLA

1000 voi

Vente à

magnifique appa

VITUS

pour votre

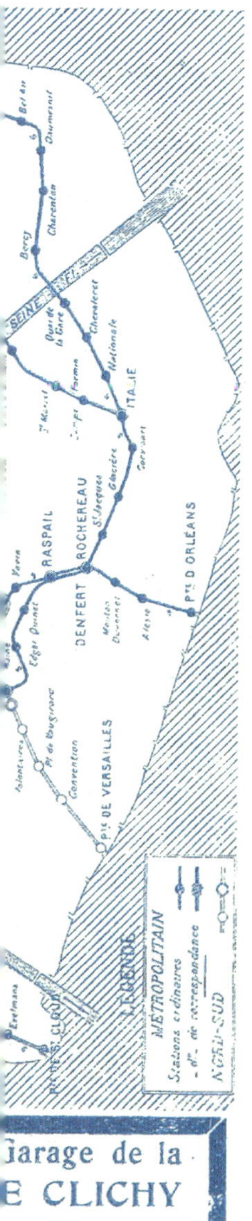

iarage de la
E CLICHY
ue Forest
PARIS

s 120 boxes

E RENAULT

t Marcadet 01-25 27-67 27-68 27-69

reil

Salon

EN PLEIN CŒUR DU
MONTPARNASSE

LE
BAR AMERICAIN
FALSTAFF

ENGLISH AMERICAN DRINKS
PORTOS CINTRA
TOUS PRODUITS D'ORIGINE
SANDWICHES

42, rue du Montparnasse, 42
Littré 51-90

Le Bœuf sur le Toit

THES - DINERS
SOUPERS DANSANTS
BAR AMERICAIN
26, rue de Penthièvre, 26
(Anjou 11-10)

Le Grand Ecart

ouvert à minuit
ORCHESTRE - DANSES
7, rue Fromentin, 7
(Trudaine 13-34)

MOULIN ROUGE Music-Hall

M. Pierre FOUCRET présente :

ELSIE JAN

dans la grande revue d'hiver

ALLO...ICI P RIS

avec

GEORGIUS
EARL LESLIE
TOSH-TWINS
DIANE BELI
RYOUX et DAND

300 artistes 00 costumes

Location : Marcadet 43-48 et 43

Legacy

In 2018, my book *French Moderne: Cocktails from the 1920s & 1930s* was published by Rizzoli New York. The volume sought to place French-inspired cocktails in their historical context.

Though originally from the United States, cocktails experienced a golden age in France during the 1920s and 1930s. This book is therefore a snapshot of the interwar period, a moment of cocktail effervescence in France, particularly in Paris.

I explore cocktails from a historical, cultural and gustatory perspective, aiming to show that far from being just a fad, cocktails were a genuine social phenomenon. With mixed drinks arriving as they did in the heyday of printed mass media, I spent several months at the Bibliothèque Historique de la ville de Paris (BHVP), poring over newspapers from these two decades.

The extreme contemporaneity of the period is fascinating! Just as in the visual arts, literature, architecture, design, and fashion, everything was in place to elevate the cocktail into one of the founding elements of this new society emerging after the trauma of 1914-1918. I examine how avant-garde movements embraced this beverage, how women – the famous *garçonnes*, with short hair, a cigarette on their lips, and a cocktail in hand – appropriated a drink previously reserved for men, and how Paris, the capital of victory, became the capital of the mixed drink. Innovation was indeed happening on our side of the Atlantic, since the United States had banned alcohol consumption during Prohibition starting in 1920.

What about a legacy? What should be done with it? If the inertia of the present does not mean the enjoyment of the past, what can such a legacy bring us? Because cocktails always reflect the spirit of their time, I sought to reinterpret these interwar creations in a modern way – cocktails that remain contemporary and vibrant precisely because they draw their strength from their history.

This inheritance from past to present allows us to offer at Cravan what we call “classics”: cocktails imagined by others in other eras, but refreshed by us for today’s palate, proving themselves eminently modern. My goal is to adapt these recipes to contemporary tastes without nostalgia, moving forward while respecting the past. These classics have endured the passage of time, enriched by stories and lives, to reach us intact. Ever accurate, they are fully part of our approach.

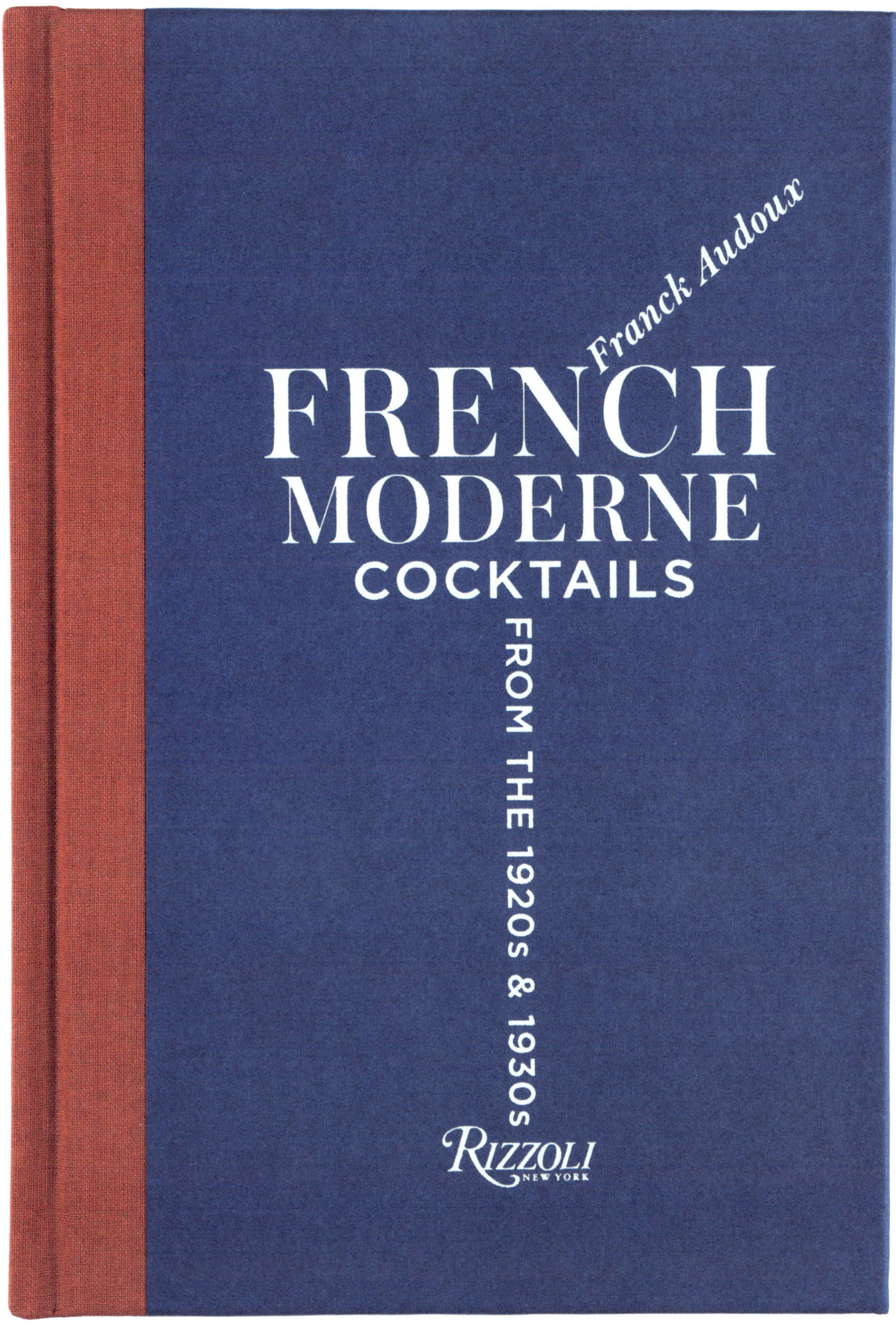
Franck Audoux
FRENCH
MODERNE
COCKTAILS
FROM THE 1920s & 1930s
RIZZOLI
NEW YORK

Courbes géométriques
Pièges à encre (inktraps)
Terminaisons droites
CRA
ABCDE
NOPQR

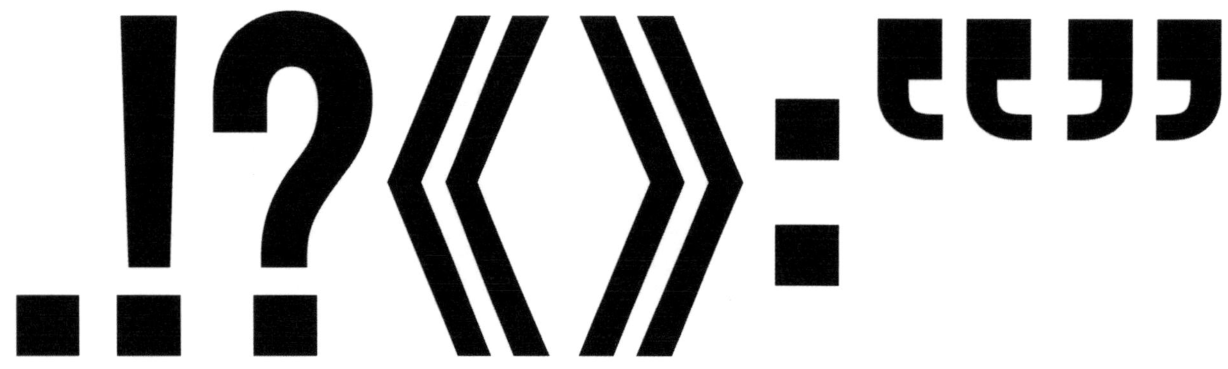
.!?《》:“”

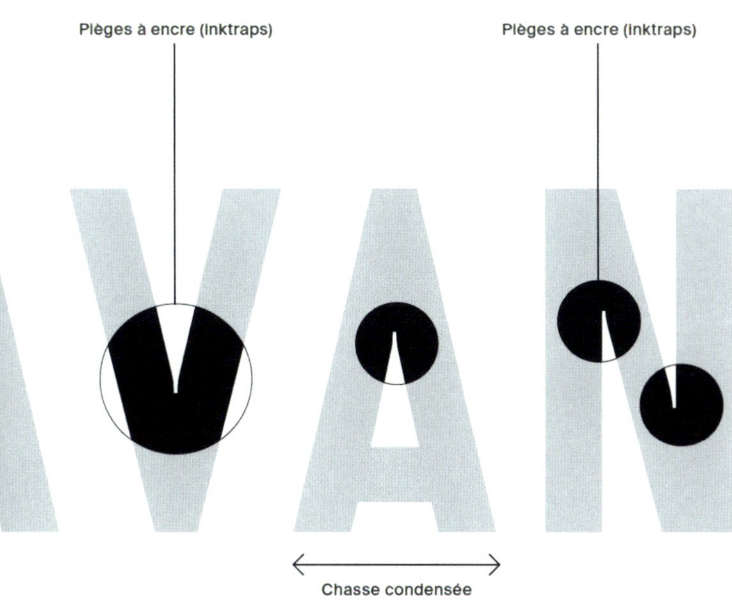

FGHIJKLM

STUVWXYZ

Letters

ABCD

NOPQR

EFGHIJKLM

STUVWXYZ

équilibre?

largeur?

Just as the great libraries of antiquity were divided into two sections, one Greek and the other Latin, the universal library virtually gathers together all the libraries of the world – of every culture, every nation, every language, and every era.

It contains not only books, but also objects scarcely resembling texts at all, things bearing only the faintest connection to what we now call literature.

It matters little that in practice we will know only an infinitesimal part of it: the world library is not a concrete institution but a working concept, a scientific tool, a reading protocol, a particular way of approaching works, an ethics of knowledge, ultimately a way of life – that of a man of letters.

William Marx,
Living in the Library of the World
Collège de France / Fayard, 2020

VICTOR DURUY
HISTOIRE DES ROMAINS
HISTOIRE DES GRECS
GÉOGRAPHIE
The Smiths
STICKERS VOL.2
DB Burkeman
United Arrows
Mark Gonzales
SPIKE JONZE BEASTIE BOYS
UNDERCOVER
KIM GORDON NO ICON

Library

In conversation with Ramy Fischler

Belgian designer Ramy Fischler is the architect of the Grand Cravan, where he completely reimagined the building on 165 Boulevard Saint-Germain and the layout of its four floors. He projected the space into the future while reintegrating elements of the original structure, with the idea of making it a bridge between several worlds: that of its origins in the 17th century, on which the project partly rests, interwoven with other settings and backdrops to provoke the unexpected in a cocktail bar – and not only of the liquid kind.

At Cravan, there is something of the tracking shot in *The Ladies Man* by Jerry Lewis and its dollhouse-like quality (though without sentimentality), a touch of Escher's grand staircase, and the architectural cross-sections of Jean-Luc Godard's *Tout va bien*.

The two staircases that lead patrons up the building serve as "true false markers" (*vrais faux repères*) that alternatively convey and disorient. The distinctive bar counters heighten the play of foregrounds and exposed backstage areas – which mimic those in a theater – giving the whole an almost playful, even surreal, labyrinthine air. Through a multitude of references drawn from the worlds of art, cinema, literature, and architecture, Franck Audoux reveals some of what inspired the creation of a place designed for the consumption of beverages.

Ramy and Franck evoke the various stages of Cravan's imaginary construction – a bar like no other, set on a prestigious boulevard that never sleeps. The risk was immense in creating an unconventional space devoted solely to cocktails and refined bar cuisine in a short time frame (less than two years).

The designer recounts how he managed to fit worlds inside other worlds, within spaces not so vast, where one can happily get lost. The conversation turns alternately to cinema in theater, philosophy in action, surrealism on the menu, wood beneath marble, humor in the glass, and a few liquids that blur one's vision.

Maison

M

FA Your scenography for *Hamlet* by Cyril Teste, which I saw at the Opéra-Comique in 2022, seems to me a key element in the conception of the Grand Cravan. On stage there was this sense of distance, of doubling the space – but above all, that décor, and behind it, the counter-décor, with its endless play of *mise en abyme* (a story within a story).

RF *Hamlet* arrived at just the right moment. Not in my first encounter with Franck – we already knew each other – but in the forging of a shared vision for this project: small in scale, yet immense in ambition. Almost magically, all those who would one day shape Cravan found themselves together one evening in the theater, seated in the same row. It reminded me of Renoir's *Rules of the Game*, when all the protagonists gather in a single room for the unraveling of the intrigue. It was already a *mise en abyme*: from the first balcony, where I sat each night with Cyril Teste, I could look down and see the entire Cravan team in a single frame. And you, Franck, wore your Cravan teddy with its name across the back. I even have a photograph of you, seated before the stage – an image deeply "Cravanesque," perhaps one of the very first.

MO And how long did Cravan take to be realized?

RF Strangely fast. We had only a few weeks to produce a sketch – it would either pass or fail. That, to me, is the essence of Cravan: it is never halfway. It is an object whole and blazing, its form, substance, and meaning inseparable. I relished the challenge – I like to play. From the outset, we leapt forward at full speed. We presented together, the three of us: Caroline [Grenthe] with the drinks, Franck with the décor, and myself with the narrative – the full strategy, united. Once launched, studies and then construction advanced with remarkable speed, carried by a rare, positive energy. In all, it took barely a year and a half, with nine months of works in the heart of Paris – exceptional! The urgency, the constraint, proved a gift: they preserved the singularity of our proposition.

The décor and its counter-décor are the skeleton of the house, just as they were in *Hamlet*'s scenography. To see the back of the set, to offer the spectator – who is also ourselves – the point of view of the actor or the camera, to cross perspectives: this way of inhabiting space and time has always fascinated me. Cyril's staging made the *mise en abyme* literal: singers and actors were visible to the audience even as they were filmed, the décor no longer only frontal. In theater and opera, distance is often used to blur perception, exaggerating textures, minimizing detail. But when cinema enters the stage, everything becomes visible – even the invisible. Actors who leave the scene remain in sight, the off-stage becomes set. Ariane Mnouchkine had already explored this "total theater," but today real-time video deepens it further.

For me as a designer, this practice is invaluable. At ENSCI-Les Ateliers, more than twenty years ago, I was already staging fictions to present my projects, small theatrical scenes as a form of design. My diploma, on public space and surveillance cameras, imagined a cinematic device much like *Hamlet*'s curtain: performers acted in front of it, then left the stage to reappear in the street or in the metro, their path followed on screen. Real or faux real time allowed me to splice fragments into new narratives. Fifteen years later, when I met Cyril, it was natural to fuse our visions. *Hamlet* became the union of two approaches to narrative, a staging in constant motion where nothing is fixed – not even the décor.

The curtain itself changes identity with each instant: transforming the set in real

FA Franck Audoux
RF Ramy Fischler
MO Marie Ottavi

time, becoming set, becoming screen. A rail, a curtain – that is enough. Radical, yet inexhaustible in its metamorphosis. I think of the scene when *Hamlet* attends his mother's wedding: first we see it frontally; then, as the curtain passes, the stage flips, revealing the reverse. The audience sees both sides of the same situation. That, too, is profoundly "Cravanesque."

Movement is the thread of my design practice: I resist fixing things in time, resist their premature obsolescence. More than ever today, there is the danger of creating places bound only to a passing "moment" – what we call a trend, a moment that grows shorter and shorter. Cravan is rooted instead in a paradox: a 17th-century house in Saint-Germain-des-Prés, the oldest in its quarter, revived with its history and spirit intact, yet injected with anachronistic décors and dissonant worlds. Guests who cross its threshold are inevitably unsettled, drawn into a fiction where the real and the unreal dissolve into one another.

FA My reference here is Jerry Lewis's *The Ladies Man*. The entire film unfolds in a house, its front cut away like a dollhouse, every room visible. There is that famous tracking shot which pulls back to reveal the whole house as a studio set, like a toy. At Cravan, the same occurs: each floor offers both décor and counter-décor, you can sip a drink in the "back" of the bar. There is demarcation, but also a sense of wandering, like in Godard's *Tout va bien*, where the camera glides from one level to another. At Cravan, each ascent to a new floor carries a trace of that. And the two staircases, structuring the skeleton of the house, bring to mind Rembrandt's *Philosopher in Contemplation* with its enigmatic spiral, or the infinite stairs of Escher where one can lose oneself forever.

MO What is the story of this house?

RF For four centuries it has passed from owner to owner. Its outer façades remain intact, yet inside almost nothing survived – save for the magnificent timber frame that holds the roof over the fourth floor. One must imagine, at its origin, a modest dwelling in an equally modest quarter, standing beside more distinguished homes.

FA So it is not a private mansion.

RF No, not one of those aristocratic *hôtels particuliers* with soaring ceilings and formal salons. Its beauty lies instead in simplicity, in the measure of the human body. It was raised by a small developer who meant to rent each floor as living quarters and the ground level as a shop. I am drawn to the history of places where I work, to the lives once lived within their walls. From these layers I weave connections, setting times, uses, and styles into dialogue.

This building, at the corner of Rue du Dragon and Boulevard Saint-Germain, stands lower than its neighbors, built later and taller. In the seventeenth century, the boulevard did not exist, but the ground floors already bustled with taverns, bookshops, apothecaries, merchants of wine and spice. Windows were scarce, façades shuttered in wood. Old engravings capture the animation of those stalls, so close to the Abbey of Saint-Germain-des-Prés.

With this renovation I wished to restore fragments of that vanished past, long effaced by successive alterations. Cravan's identity emerged through a layering of histories: exposed beams, limestone floors, lime-washed walls – set against contemporary décor that nods to the world of Parisian cocktail bars. We sought to make a collage, at times pushed toward the absurd, so that each floor speaks a

language of its own, almost unreal, yet true to the vision we held for Cravan. Though visitors may not discern every aesthetic choice, a secret logic runs through it. References hide within the décor, nested like mismatched boxes.
As one ascends the floors, a narrative intensity gathers. The ground floor, made to resemble the most ordinary Parisian bistro, begins this journey – disorienting, yet never forbidding. To step through Cravan's door is to believe one has entered a neighborhood café, when in truth the visitor is already immersed in a stage set, a performative, playful unreality that ushers them into the maison's world.

FA All the more since the ground floor is itself a replica of the Cravan in the sixteenth arrondissement – an Art Nouveau bar, discreet and unostentatious. Collage is the very essence of the project. To make Cravan live, as with the cocktail, is to assemble disparate elements – one might even say, to collage them. Our method, our juxtapositions, are not hidden but proudly visible, deliberate, almost theatrical.

RF Yes, it is truly a collage, more than an assemblage, precisely because the breaks between décors are laid bare. The "stage backdrop" that runs through every floor reminds us that the illusion is total, and nothing is real. Even if each space is crafted with perfection – the parquet seeming as old as the walls, the materials noble and authentic – the juxtapositions deny any illusion of historic truth.

To slip behind the décor is to realize that the setting, elegant and welcoming though it appears, is in fact unreal. Yet at the same time, it opens another perspective – one that is real. Whether seated on one side of the décor or the other, we are all actors and spectators in a play that repeats without end – Franck evoked Escher's impossible perspectives, or a Parisian version of *Lost in Translation*.

FA The rupture you speak of – does it return often in your projects?

RF Yes. There are several reasons for it, though I don't always theorize them – it comes rather instinctively. When a space feels too narrow, and I sense the need to expand its visual field, I trick the eye by breaking it open, scattering perspectives to create passages, vistas, and secret corners that enrich the experience. I offer more to see and to live than what is strictly asked of me. This multiplication of space also reflects the hybrid nature of our times: the need for modularity and agility in a world constantly shifting, challenged by the lure of virtual experience. These crossing forces compel us to rethink how we imagine and shape the places where we live and play.

Because I am a designer before I am an interior architect, I approach space as if it were an object. An object can be turned in every direction; it has no hidden face, it can be shifted, overturned. I like the idea that certain designs – Cravan among them – are not fixed, but transient, meant to transform, visible from every side. I do not thrive in places that seem frozen in time, especially when they are meant for pleasure, escape, disconnection. We return here to the theatrical experience: for the spectator it feels ephemeral, even though it may be repeated night after night in exactly the same way. Cravan carries this same sense of movement, of displacement – at once unstable, disconcerting, and surprising – yet bound together in a stable, enduring identity.

FA This idea of rupture, of collage, creates a multiplicity of fictions. At Cravan – which, after all, is not such a large house – one feels, because of these ruptures, almost lost. It isn't a

labyrinth, yet something of the labyrinth lingers. Clients sometimes ask: *"But didn't I take a different staircase a moment ago?"* There is this sense of being inside the set, the backstage, the real-false. The first floor illustrates it well: you can drink a glass while seated on a stool behind the cube at the back of the bar, in a seventeenth-century décor. These are sensations the clients – I almost said spectators – can feel.

RF We are all at once users and spectators. And that is precisely why I believe we are always in need of scenography, of *mise en scène*, of "theatricalizing" our daily lives. Our imagination can animate what is fixed. Place wheels on furniture that never moves, and suddenly, in a sense, it becomes mobile. That is the case, for example, with the library on the second floor.

We have grown accustomed to speed, to continual change; we struggle to appreciate slowness, contemplation. Fragmenting space, creating dissonance, is a strategy to sharpen attention, to cross perspectives, to disrupt rhythm and destination, to invite accidents along the way, to shatter monotony with the unexpected. Even without naming it, we know: one does not live the same experience in a bar where chairs are neatly aligned, where the room is harmonious and predictable, as in Cravan, where obliqueness, rupture, and displacement loosen our bearings and compel us to reconsider our very presence in space.

MO There's a risk in that, isn't there?

RF It was very risky.

FA Yet it still belongs to that idea of disorientation: offering something different, breaking with the norm – but without being iconoclastic. That's what I try to do with cocktails as well.

RF To break the "optimal efficiency" of a place is indeed risky – but that is life. If we chose these *métiers*, it was not to follow rules, to answer the same question in the same way each time. And yet, when it works, it works tenfold. These dissonances, these ruptures, these fragmentations – they give the place a rhythm, a temporality unlike any other bar. That was our aim.

MO It could even evoke a video game, depending on one's generation…

RF Indeed. Certain spatial configurations inevitably reference gaming culture. Today, I must reckon with the pull of virtual realities, these captivating worlds that inevitably alter how we perceive the real. Cravan is anchored in reality – you drink cocktails there, you live real interactions, real emotions. But in *Minecraft* too, you feed yourself, you build worlds, you shape environments, you form communities. In virtual worlds you can do anything: blend settings, change lives, reinvent yourself.

For the generation growing up caught between reality and fiction, the real and the virtual, choosing to go out no longer holds the same meaning as it did for those who only had fêtes and bars for sociability and pleasure. The real cannot afford to become less accessible, less surprising, less exhilarating than the virtual.

MO Have we grown almost afraid, even suspicious, of the real?

RF There is indeed a risk – that reality becomes so codified, so conventional, that future generations will retreat to the virtual to release pressure, to break rules, to revel. It's a dystopian vision, yet not so far from truth. A bar exists to anchor us again in

reality – in the sense of fête, of shared pleasure, of alchemy between scent, touch, taste, and the serendipity of encounter. And yet, this hybridization of life, spectacle, and experience reminds me of certain formats that marked me deeply.

I've spoken already of Ariane Mnouchkine, who invented this free, borderless theatrical practice. The set transforms before the audience; actors become servers at intermission; the wings are at the entrance, visible to all, so that you glimpse backstage before seeing the stage. Her earliest works, which I never saw, unfolded in apartments, where you followed the story room by room. It was the beginning of what we now call immersive theater – *Sleep No More*, *Queen of the Night*, born in New York. In these performative formats, the visitor becomes part of the spectacle. The whole building becomes a stage; the audience wanders; the actors too. Depending on which door you open, you encounter a different story. To me, this surpasses video games, but it remains inaccessible to many. I don't have the power to democratize such costly, precarious formats, but I try to shape spaces that can cradle them. Cravan belongs to this lineage.

MO Liquor, too, helps loosen the performance…

RF True – drink and intoxication foster disorientation, surrender. We designed Cravan with this gradual shift in perception in mind, as the night extends. On the first floor, I had seventeenth-century paintings reproduced – works so faithful that we sought out the finest copyists. They melt seamlessly into the cracked wood-paneling. Yet I asked the painters to render them slightly blurred – what Photoshop calls a directional blur. To reproduce this by hand was no simple feat. I wanted to instill into the painting itself a trembling uncertainty, to amplify that budding intoxication with graphic games – sometimes hypnotic, like the mirrored screen cloaking the bar. When the rooms are full, when bodies mingle, eyes meet, guests drift from one floor to another – up one staircase, down the other – the disorientation, the threshold between reality and fiction, occurs on its own. Each time I return to Cravan, I search for that sensation of wandering, of rediscovering it as though for the very first time.

FA William Marx has written much about invisible libraries, imaginary libraries, the physical and the mental space of them. Earlier you mentioned wheels on a fixed bookcase, a stool that becomes a pedestal, transformed into a table. At Cravan you've multiplied these crossings of object and function. Modularity seems constant in your work, no?

RF You mean the lectern-tables I designed for the library on the second floor. They are simple wooden tables, clad in a thin skin of metal, able to host books or serve as seating. Unlike the furniture on the other floors, this space of reading was conceived as a place in movement – to host a flux of events, to ward off monotony. The pieces of furniture were built to move easily, in contrast to the almost institutional presence of the bookshelves – the aura of stillness that books can impose.

At Cravan, the library is a place of gathering, of *fête*, never solemn. Books are laid open on the tables, accessible at a glance, never far from a glass. The lectern-table is an idea I developed at the Villa Medici in 2010. A wink to my Roman past, when I grafted lecterns onto the cafeteria tables designed by Richard Peduzzi – prototypes of those I have recreated here.

The French Revolution and the seizure of noble libraries had endowed the Academy with extraordinary volumes. During my Roman year, I immersed myself in them: Diderot and d'Alembert's original encyclopedias, Leonardo's first treatises on architecture. I wandered archives and inventories, weaving my readings into thematic fanzines for visitors. Already it was collage – a technique not new to me. At Cravan, there are no fanzines, but this furniture allows one to offer a book to view, and replace it at will.

This library, too, has two layers: a metal arch dedicated to Rizzoli editions, and a more traditional – though not entirely – array of a hundred rare books, which we delighted in selecting during construction, now freely available to our guests. The wheeled pieces, Franck, you move them often, reshuffling their contents. The arch itself, though on wheels, never moves. Clients ask if we shift it often and believe me when I say it came down from the third floor! It takes only wheels, even under the most monumental of objects, to make them appear mobile in the mind.

MO You work a great deal with the notion of use…

RF Indeed – I even have a "bureau of uses" in the studio. We often begin projects with substance before form, questioning not only present functions but the ways we might inhabit the world tomorrow. I believe profoundly in the ability of objects to shape life, to lift or lower spirits. I myself am deeply sensitive to my surroundings; I react differently to the objects that encircle me – their beauty, their utility, the intelligence of their making.

When I design a place or an object, I inhabit it in the mind of its user. At Cravan, rarely, I did not need to imagine another's perspective: Caroline, Franck, and I were already our own most demanding clients.

FA And to conclude, Ramy, what is a "House" to you? An imaginary space, a place of use?

RF The notion of the House – with a capital "H" – is what defines the Grand Cravan. A House is the center of gravity for a brand, the place where everything is infused and from which everything radiates. It is a vessel of meaning, of references, a toolbox for decades to come. To shine outward, Cravan needed its base – and that base could only be in Saint-Germain-des-Prés, historic crossroads of literature, of *fête*, of the Parisian art of living, inseparable from its identity.

I have worked with centennial houses – Chanel, Ruinart, Dom Pérignon. But to be at the dawn of a new House is another creative matter entirely. Every material, every form, every object, every use – we shape with coherence, guided by a narrative thread that is written even as it inscribes itself into the history of the brand. The future will be the judge of our audacity.

A HOUSE IS THE CENTER OF GRAVITY FOR A BRAND,

THE PLACE WHERE EVERYTHING IS INFUSED AND FROM WHICH EVERYTHING RADIATES.

M

Measure

- Got any records?

- Yes. What do you want? Some Bach…

- No. It's too late. Bach is for
8 o'clock in the morning
… a Brandenberg at 8 o'clock in the morning
is wonderful.

- Some Mozart? Beethoven?

- Too early. Mozart is 8 o'clock at night.
Beethoven is very profound music.
Beethoven is for midnight.

Jean-Luc Godard,
Le Petit Soldat,
1963

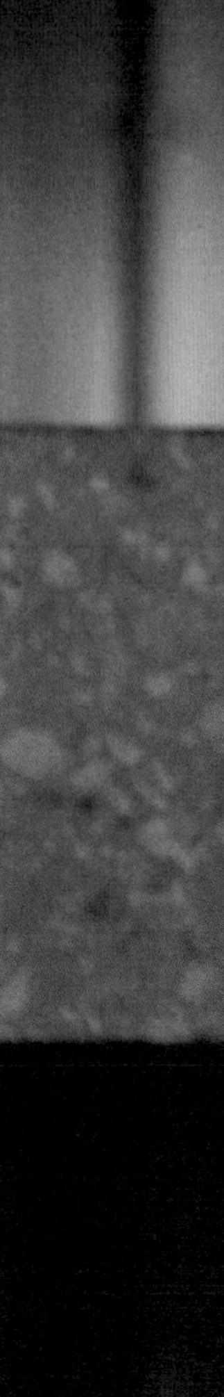

QUAD
bass
treble
slope
controls
filter
← mon
mon →
stereo
disc
radio 1
radio 2
tape
cancel
5k
7k
10k
QUAD 405

M

Music

C
COCKTAILS
PRÊTS À SERVIR
C
R
A
V
A
N
NEGRONI
21% VOL.
SERVIR FRAIS
50 CL

N

Negroni

Like for many in the bar world, the Negroni remains one of my favorite cocktails, with an apparent simplicity that opens onto true aromatic complexity.

It's also always the first cocktail I order when visiting a bar for the first time. The Negroni is the benchmark that tells me a lot about the establishment's style, depending on the ingredients that are used and the way it is served.

I must admit that today's interpretations are sometimes too sweet for my taste. That's why, when I came across the *Cocktails de Paris* book from 1929, my attention was drawn to a recipe called Tunnel. The book is a collection of recipes created by bartenders and Parisian personalities for various competitions held between 1928 and 1929. The Tunnel, which won the grand prize at the Bartenders' Championship on February 2, 1929, was already a twist on the classic created ten years earlier. With the addition of dry vermouth in equal parts to gin, I found there an interesting path toward enjoying a drier cocktail than what I was usually served.

So I started from that recipe and adapted it, not to reinterpret a classic, but to make it more relevant to today's palate. I kept the classic Negroni structure of three equal parts and deliberately chose easily accessible ingredients. Our recipe therefore consists of one-third gin, one-third dry vermouth, and the final third made up of more bitter-than-sweet vermouth.

The result is a drier, more bitter Negroni, because I wanted once again to enjoy a truly aperitif-style cocktail. Less sweet, with a dry finish designed to whet the appetite.

Our version of the Negroni is now part of our range of ready-to-serve bottled classic cocktails, which we produce with the help and expertise of the Alsatian distillery Nusbaumer. With its 75 years of experience, we also created our own gin to best suit our recipe, a London dry with a citrusy finish, as I used to express a grapefruit zest in the craft version. Already diluted with spring water, it only needs to be served chilled.

For me, our Negroni is the perfect example of how to adapt a classic. While keeping its original character, we've given it a new gustatory dimension:
Drier. Bitter. Better.

より辛口に より苦く
DRIER BITTER
より美味しい
BETTER

Look around you, in the environment in which you live. You are immersed in the external world by means of the light it gives you. The study of luminous phenomena is therefore essential; it is what we call optics.

Traditionally, one distinguishes between “geometrical” optics and “physical” optics. The first considers only the path of light rays through air and transparent media. It makes it possible to imagine and build instruments of observation such as mirrors, magnifying glasses, microscopes, binoculars, and telescopes. It does not, except in special cases, concern itself with the actual nature of light. Physical optics, on the other hand, always takes into account the structure of light, which is a vibration propagating through the void at a speed of 300,000 kilometers a second.

The Great Book of Science in Full Color

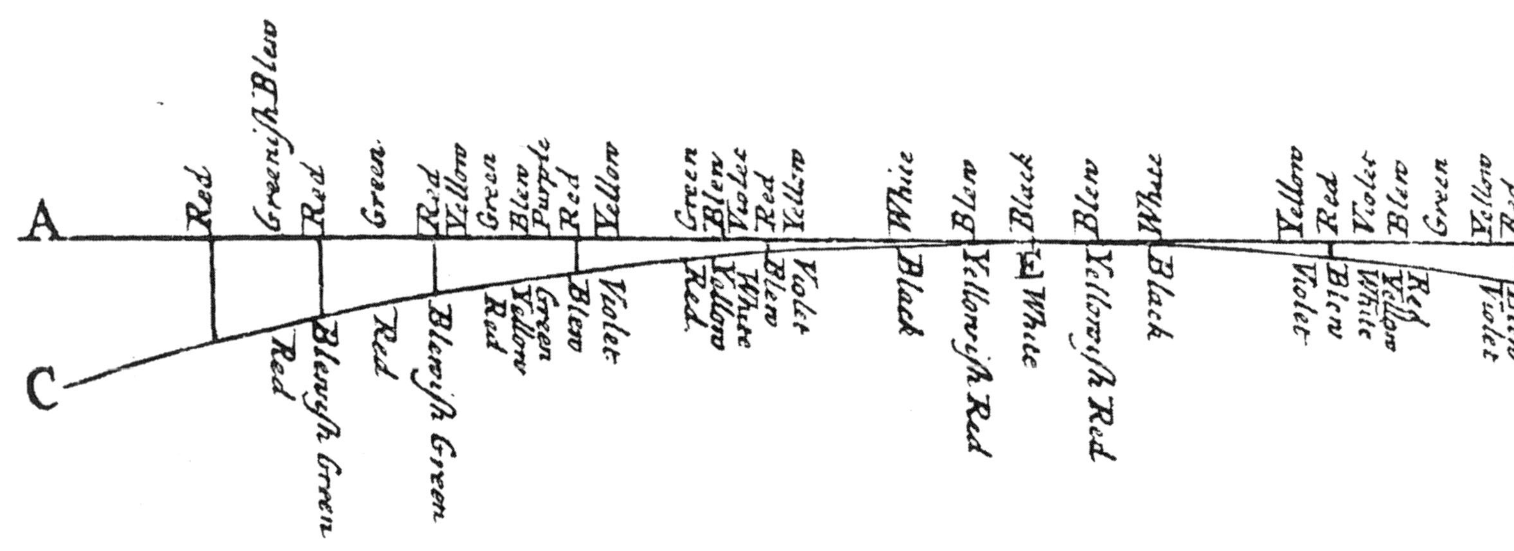

YELLOW
GREENISH YEL.
YEL.GREEN
GREEN
EM.GREEN
G.C.G.BLUE
G.C.BLUE
G.BLUE
CYAN BLUE 1
CYAN BLUE 2
ULT.BLUE NAT
ULT.BLUE ARTF
VIOLET
PURPLE
RED PURPLE
CARMINE
SP.RED
VERMILION
RED LEAD
ORANGE
ORANGE YELLOW
Yellow
Red
Green
Red
Greenish Blew
Red
Greenish Red
Pale Red
B
Red
Blewish Green
Red
Blewish Green
Red
D
O

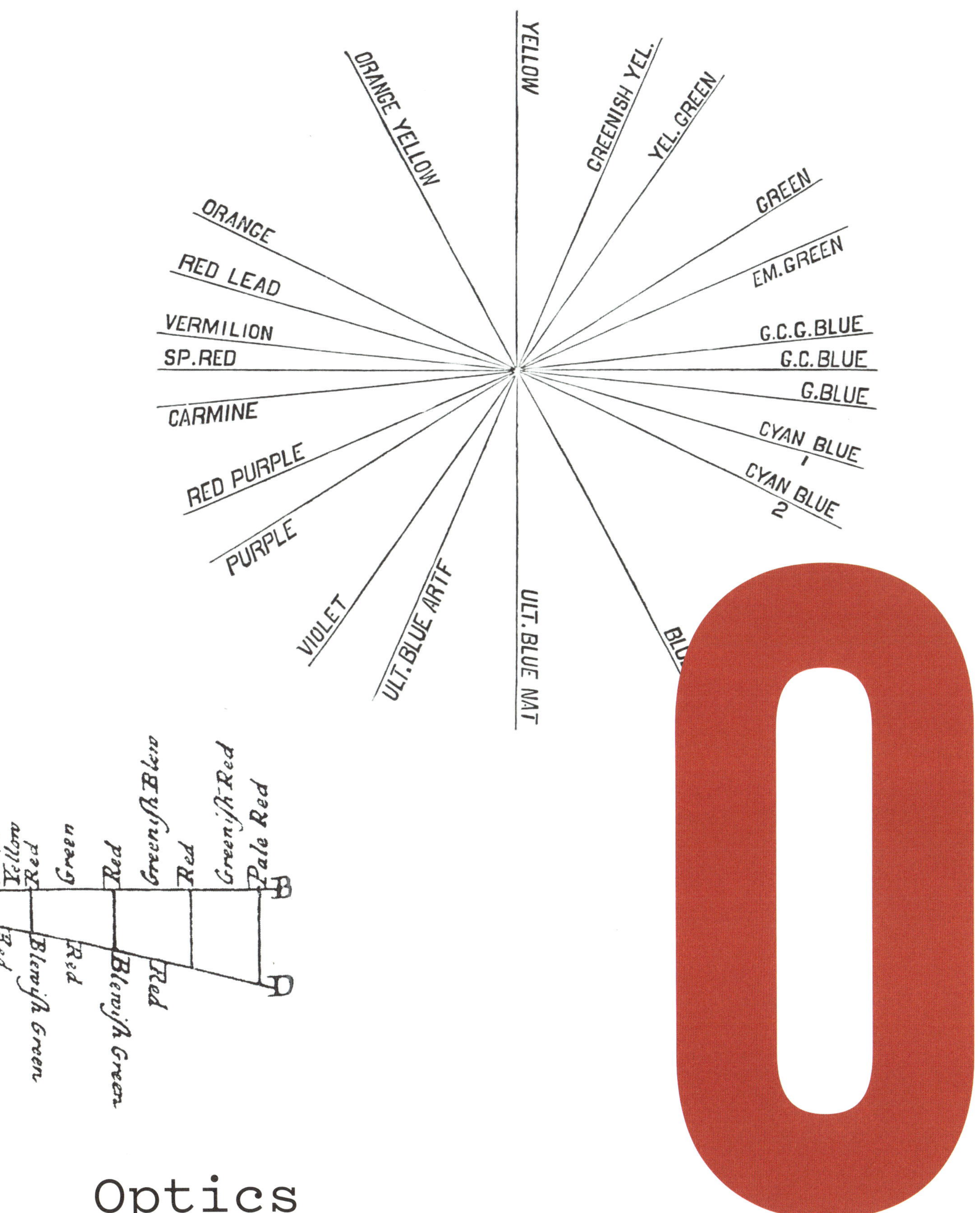

Optics

4h – Square Heart / Neo Seven

5h – Lil' Darlin' / Count Basie

6h – Who loves the Sun / The Velvet Underground

7h – Lovesick Blues / Hank Williams

8h – Kawasaki / Jane Birkin

~~9h –~~

9h – Bluebird / Wings

10h – A little lost / Arthur Russel

~~11h – Pocket full of~~

11h – Pocketful of Rainbows / Elvis Presley

12h – Prelúdio Ao Coração / Baden Powell

13h – Autobahn / Kraftwerk

14h – Desolation Row / Bob Dylan

15h – Wiederstehe nach der Sünde / Nicolas Godin

16h – I thought the World of You / Lewis Balone

17h- Cosmic Dancer - T-Rex

18 h- Izaura / João Gilberto

19h- I'm Glad you're Mine / Al Green

20 h- So good to be at Trouble / Unknown Mortal Orchestra

21h- Step by Step / Alan Braxe + Dj Falcon

22h- Bad Habits / Steve Lacy

23h- So in Love / Curtis Mayfield

24h- L'alcool / Serge Gainsbourg

1h - Ancora Tu / Lucio Battisti

2h- Solo / Franck Ocean

3h- Fantino / Sebastian Tellier

P

Playlist

4h – Ferber endormi / Christophe

5h – Talking / Haruomi Hosono

6h – Homesickness Part 2 / Tsegue-Maryam Guebrou

7h – Wonderful / The Beach Boys

8h – Ah Melody / Serge Gainsbourg

9h – Venus / Frankie Avalon

10h – The makings of you / Curtis Mayfield

11h – Jerry Garcia Band / Rubin and Cherise

12h – What's going on (rythm 'N' strings mix) / Marvin Gaye

Marvin Gaye

Marvin Gaye

13h – This will be our year / The Zombies

14h – On the level – Mac de Marco

15h – Tomorrow / Wings

16h – Young and innocent days / The Kinks

17h – Tette e antenne / Ennio Morricone

18h – L'appuntamento / Ornella Vanoni

19h – Emozioni / Lucio Battisti

20h - Boku Wa Chotto - / Haruomi Hosono

21h - With my face on the floor / Emitt Rhodes

22h - Lying has to stop / Soft Hair

23h - Present / Yukihiro Takahashi

24h - Construçao / Chico Buarque

1h - On dreams / Sons of Raphael

2h - Turiya and Ramakrishna - Alice Coltrane

3h - On the other Ocean - David Behrman

By **Christian Mazzala**
founding member of Phoenix

FANT
CE VOLUME EST VENDU 35 CENT AU LIEU DE 65
10.45PM
Talking
12:15PM
Homesickness
6.00PM
Wonderful
Beach Boys
CARTE
C
Légende
Key

CRAVAN
Q
Quote

A few precious drops of liquid are poured with expert precision into a Champagne coupe.

A carefully measured gesture, bringing to life an extraordinary project born from the combined imagination of Franck Audoux at Cravan and Vincent Chaperon at Dom Pérignon. Two men who, through just a handful of encounters, managed to weave a dialogue fueled by their growing complicity; two creators facing the question of liquid and the emotions it can convey.

Very soon, the idea of a collaboration between Cravan and Dom Pérignon, between cocktail and Champagne, began to take shape. Franck suggested that Vincent venture into an entirely new logic for Champagne: that of blends and associations. Tasting a version of the Royal imagined by Franck, Vincent immediately glimpsed Champagne from a new angle and perceived the possibility of "expanding its territory of creation." Rightly so, since for Franck Audoux, a "cocktail functions like an open window."

Vincent embraced the risk. The idea was to attempt new additions of flavor to Dom Pérignon in order to "reveal its deeper facets. … My quest," adds Vincent Chaperon, "is to look at my Champagnes from a new angle, under a new light."

Royal

Stretching and Elevation

When crafting his cocktails, Franck Audoux seeks the "precision of aromas." Vincent speaks in similar terms, evoking the principle of "harmony in tension."

Even if this truth must ultimately emerge on the palate, in the taste and especially the texture of his wines, the aesthetic line is undeniably the same. But the similarities go further. In Franck's art of blending, Vincent recognized an extension of his own creative approach.

Indeed, he conceives his pursuit of harmony through assemblage as a never-ending quest.

Every addition – from the grape to the Champagne, whether structure or texture, however infinitesimal – must complete the canvas of flavors, heightening emotion. The external elements proposed by Franck could thus enhance the original assemblage and take it further. In Vincent's own words, they would "underline, stretch, prolong."

More concretely, and in line with the singular *savoir-faire* of Champagne, the addition of an external element also recalls for Vincent the traditional *liqueur de dosage* added before corking.

Clearly, this project with Cravan does not depart from the creative principles and craftsmanship of Dom Pérignon. The collaboration therefore focused on the Royal, a Champagne-based cocktail that has featured on Cravan's menu since its opening and perfectly reflects Franck's taste for purity and refinement.

The Champagne is complemented by the addition of a discreet flavor. For Franck, it is about "highlighting the taste of Champagne through the addition of a vegetal note," obtained by a process of infusion. Dom Pérignon here reveals its intensity and precision.

For Vincent Chaperon, the exercise is fascinating in that it demonstrates Dom Pérignon's ability to react while always remaining true to itself.

"We are no longer speaking of a cocktail," he summarizes, but rather of an "extension of Champagne" designed to reveal it.

Dom Pérignon, almost amplified, strengthens its personality through this encounter. For the creators, the success lies in the fact that the association of flavors revealing Dom Pérignon takes place directly in the glass rather than coming from outside.

That is why they chose to describe it as a "liquid-to-liquid pairing," in contrast with the classic food-and-wine pairing.

A Moment Anticipated and Suspended

On the evening of May 22, 2023, the first guests were gathered to discover the fruit of the collaboration between Franck and Vincent, between Cravan and Dom Pérignon.

The bar barely held the twenty or so guests, arranged around the large rectangular table. Seating was free, meetings improvised, exchanges unexpected. Worlds collided: graphic designers and artists rubbed shoulders with wine experts, sommeliers, and specialized journalists. Preconceived notions instantly dissolved, giving way to a collective state of receptiveness.

The duo, presenting themselves together for the first time, had much to do with it. Demonstrating both complicity and authority, they set the tone for discovery. Months later, among participants, memories of that memorable evening remain vivid, fully embodying the power of the encounter Franck had long wished for.

The evening of May 22 embodied a sense of community – diverse, yet united by the same thirst for discovery. The surprise of the participants at this union was palpable.

Journalist Alicia Dorey spoke of a logic of "irreconcilable worlds," which sommelier Paz Levinson highlighted as "the freedom of creators who take risks."

It was a process of breaking down barriers of knowledge, surprising yet profoundly enriching for this collaboration.

Artistic Dimensions

Taking a more conceptual turn, the evening also gave artist Saâdane Afif the opportunity to introduce to the discussion the notion of the infra-mince, first imagined by Marcel Duchamp and later further elaborated by curator Thierry Davila. The relevance was obvious, as the tasting of the creations revealed an extreme subtlety.

Thierry Davila spoke of an "extreme tenuity," a lack of substance or heft where an imperceptible change can lead to great upheaval. Subtle additions revealed new aspects of Dom Pérignon, even disorienting some, such as Alicia Dorey, who confessed she was "not always certain of distinguishing the Champagne from its augmented version."

The difference was infinitesimal, and yet it sufficed to provoke change. Returning to Davila's words, one could use his expression to define the infra-mince: "producing intensities by subtraction." Indeed, it was about levels of intensity, of degrees, of depths, of shifting dimensions.

A New Temporality

The collaboration proved even more convincing in its exploration of temporality. Dom Pérignon requires a long tasting time, a necessary wait to reveal its many aesthetic dimensions. Franck's approach partly reduced this temporal dimension.

The chosen additions entered into resonance with the wine's structure. The result: revealing flavors and textures already present in Dom Pérignon within the time frame of a cocktail. The unveiling became faster, almost instantaneous. Thus, the fusion of Franck's and Vincent's universes managed to create a temporal instant apart. In the words of Vincent Chaperon, "through the Royal, time expands."

Nicolas Chatenier

In 1955, ITV, the nascent British private television network, commissioned Orson Welles to create a 26-episode series, to be broadcast every two weeks, entitled *Around the World with Orson Welles*. Despite the promise of its title, the series would cover only European locations, and of the 26 planned episodes, only six were completed: *The Basque Countries / La Pelote Basque / Revisiting Vienna / London / Saint-Germain-des-Prés / Spain - The Bullfight*.

At that time – what critics would later call his first European period, lasting from 1947 to 1955 – Orson Welles was indeed an exile in Europe, but not a stateless man. He had left Hollywood in the middle of editing *Macbeth*, yet he had not severed ties with the American public. Quite the contrary: his many European projects were openly intended to replenish his finances in order to return to Hollywood and pursue new ventures, while evading potential creditors.

And if he agreed to make what he called "travel essays on film," it was because he hoped these programs would be shown in the United States, allowing him to send word back home to his fellow countrymen. Moreover, television was a new and rapidly expanding medium that fascinated Welles – who saw it as "illustrated radio." A synthesis of cinema and radio, it offered him another means of satisfying his passion for storytelling.

Orson Welles… Saint-Germain-des-Prés… Le Vieux Colombier… Spanish dancing…
Thus begins, in the form of an investigation not unlike *Citizen Kane*, the 26-minute episode devoted to Saint-Germain-des-Prés. Here we find Welles, tireless traveler, wandering through the postwar bohemian quarter, crossing paths with Jean Cocteau and Juliette Gréco, and interviewing Raymond Duncan (Isadora's brother) at his *Akademia*. It is a true postcard from that Parisian "village," where youth lived in cellars to the rhythm of jazz, and where the password was *existentialism*, even if Jean-Paul Sartre himself wondered what his philosophical concept was doing in a bar besides serving as decoration.

Yet the episode is also fascinating for Welles's formal freedom. He included in it footage that was not his own but taken from *Le Désordre*, a 1947 short film by Jacques Baratier depicting the colorful fauna of Saint-Germain-des-Prés in the aftermath of the war. Thus we find images of Juliette Gréco, high priestess of bohemia, singing among the ruins of Paris; scenes from *Le Tabou*, the cellar discovered by Gréco herself; that "center of organized madness" in Boris Vian's words. Other shots were taken from the Basque episode or from the Spanish one. Post-synchronization was almost systematic, and the use of a body double in place of Welles at various moments fooled no one.

He incorporated all of this into the edit – none of which he would have time to finish himself. He left for New York to play *King Lear*, without leaving a forwarding address. In a 1958 *Cahiers du Cinéma* interview, Welles explained:

"Experimenting is the only thing that excites me… I am not in ecstasy before art; I am in ecstasy before human function… It is the act that interests me, not the result."

This episode, far more than a mere "exercise in style," remains a magnificent black-and-white postcard of Saint-Germain-des-Prés, signed by Orson Welles.

Saint-Germain des-Prés

In conversation with Vincent Chaperon

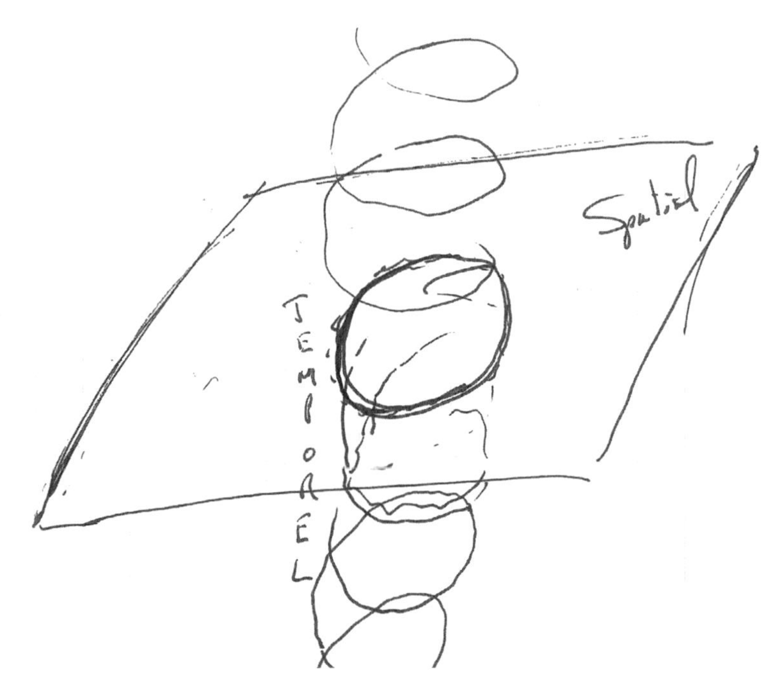

The historic abbey of Dom Pérignon, in Hautvillers, in the Marne region, sets the scene for the conversation. The tasting takes place around a long Benedictine table, in the monks' ancient sanctuary founded in the seventh century.

The meeting between Franck Audoux and Vincent Chaperon, Dom Pérignon's Cellar Master, focuses on a form, a movement, and an idea:

Spiral

REVEAL, ELEVATE, ACCENTUATE, CONCENTRATE.

Champagne and cocktail creators are sorcerers, as well as storytellers and chemists, who attempt to prolong time and make the moment last. Franck Audoux therefore seeks "to make the end the beginning, and the beginning the end." The idea of proximity and resonance between the two activities, making Champagne and making cocktails, guided their collaboration. The immediacy of the cocktail, on one hand, and the slow process that leads to the Champagne *cuvée* on the other. Equilibrium and harmony came up in movement as much as in conversation. Tension guided the research. Certain words became essential: reveal, elevate, accentuate, concentrate. The almost philosophical approach of Vincent Chaperon is at the heart of this fascinating interview: "For us, everything is built on tension, in the blend and the creation," he asserts. "We play on opposites, on contrasts, on complementarities. We extend, we stretch this liquid as much as possible in its construction. It's not spatial, because it remains within the volume of a glass, but on the inside, there are times and spaces, sensorial tensions, and we know that constructing it in this way guarantees expansion over time and a prolonged experience of the moment in tasting. We know there will be a back and forth between the immediate and the long term."

FA **I'd like to talk again about the maturation time, which I could almost oppose to that of the cocktail, which, for me, is linked to the momentary. If cinema is about making time visible, as we discussed with Dominique Païni, your work is about making a drinkable experience of time.**

VC Making it visible and making it drinkable, that's nice. For us, it's time experienced and time projected, both over the duration, but also in the moment. In this sense, it's not completely opposed to what you're looking for because in the end, the tasting is momentary. One of my main preoccupations is to succeed in unfolding the instantaneous, unfolding the moment. You once said to me: "I try to make the end the beginning, and the beginning the end." We come back to this notion of the spiral. You work with the instantaneous, but at the same time you seek a continuity, a length, a repetition.

FA **The Royal, as I've interpreted it, is a way of prolonging time.**

VC That's right. At Dom Pérignon, we're seeking an unfolding. We've been working for over ten years on folding things up and organizing layers to create the moment when they can unfold. There are several ways to unfold time to create a space-time, because we are well aware that this time is of variable geometry. We are seeking to create moments that relate to memory. Christian Dior said: "Of civilizations, only the perishable will remain." That's where we are, in this perishable moment of the immaterial. This is the great human paradox.

For example, take a 2004 Vintage released in 2012 and a 2004 Plénitude 2 Vintage that has just been released (we are in January 2023). So, the same juice, the same blend with more aging on the one hand, and more maturation on the other. Tasting obliges us to project because we are not comparing them at the same stage, even though they are the same age. This is where temporality takes on a variable geometry. Since 2004, we've been tasting them at the same time. Therefore, today, they are both 19 years old, but they aren't at the same moment in their life because one of them has matured and the other has aged.

To understand where Plénitude 2 wants to go, we must project in order to compare its potential and its trajectory. The Vintage is already at a more advanced moment in its life, not in terms of years, but in potentiality of energy. There is something of the future and of the past in the moment. It makes me think of a phrase by the architect John Pawson: "If our interest in the future is really the desire for a present which satisfies us - physically, visually and psychologically - can we develop perpetually interesting forms that exist outside the forces of time and fashion? This, I believe, is what the aesthetic of simplicity, with its vast and paradoxical potential for richness and sensuality, offers." He's seeking simplicity, the capacity to define a lasting present that projects into the future. For him, there's no history of fashion. It's not in fashion that we will find lasting pleasure. It's in the capacity to define forms and aesthetics that endure through time… Simplicity and precision, that is what endures through everything. They should be quite easily accessible.

What's truly fascinating is that they ought to speak to us – for if they pass through us, they call upon our most evident and most profound humanity. At times, they're a little blurred, hidden by the world.

FA **Hence the importance of revealing. You often say: reveal, repeat, accentuate, elevate.**

VC Revelation makes me think of light.

FA Franck Audoux
VC Vincent Chaperon
MO Marie Ottavi

From time to time, one must illuminate. Things cannot be explained – they are felt. It's only a matter of finding that instant of illumination, like the flash of a photograph. That's what I seek in experience. What Dom Pérignon brings to gastronomy is light. Gastronomy helps Dom Pérignon to reveal itself – and we, in turn, bring it light, because Champagne, to me, is light. There is something alchemical about it, for light is the elevation of matter.

FA I take a similar approach when working with exceptional wines or spirits. My task is indeed to reveal, to elevate, to sublimate – or rather, to set things in perspective and extend them further. I always compare it to the work of a goldsmith: I'm trying to move the needle.

VC When I first met you, I was struck by your approach – both cultural and historical – to your craft. The Royal was a kind of revelation that allowed me to see my own creation in a new light. My quest is to understand my product as deeply as possible – and that's what's marvelous. My product is an ingredient, and it still surprises me, because I do not know it fully. When I taste a grape, I know I'm not seeing everything. There are things revealed, in the scientific sense of the word. In our grapes, we have aromatic precursors that are invisible to the senses – they emerge only through fermentation. They're there, yet we neither smell nor taste them.

FA Time – and thus movement!

VC To me, they're inseparable.

FA Earlier, we offered people the taste of lived time. You just spoke of light, like the flash of a photograph.

VC The light of revelation.

FA The time of photography isn't a frozen one – it's time in motion. That notion of movement is essential, always within the idea of unfolding and revealing. Movement – and tension, too.

VC Tension is what binds things together. The image that comes to mind is the universe itself. Everything that happens mirrors the great movement of the cosmos, which is forever expanding. In space, time, and motion, the variables resonate – they speak to one another, and are therefore connected. There is a phenomenon of temporal expansion. Life is precisely that: a story of expansion through time, or of the time of expansion. And everything is linked – everything relates. There are forces, curves of energy, tensions, and polarities that create spaces, which themselves generate time. My way of bringing all this forth – like an architect, a creator, or a designer – is to build through tension.

FA Yes, it's extremely important for cocktails to have this tension, which is, for me, the style of the person who created these cocktails. Style as the true expression of what this person was thinking.

VC A way of organizing, like architects with lines. Tension is the line of perspective between two poles. It's what defines a direction, a style; it creates a space and an energy. For us, everything is built upon tension, in the blend and the creation. We play on opposites, contrasts, and complementarities. We extend, we stretch this liquid as much as possible in its construction. It's very conceptual. It's not spatial, because it remains within the volume of a glass, but on the inside, there are times and spaces, sensorial tensions, and we know that constructing it in this way guarantees expansion over time and a prolonged experience of the moment in tasting. We know we will observe a back and forth between the immediate and the long term. In any case, for sure, we're betting, but that's what generally happens. Your work gives the product more integrity; it takes the product to another place. This is the mystery of creation. I imagine there's a sort of brilliance, an understanding of the product that comes from your knowledge, and from your work, which gives you an intimate relationship with it. You manage to find that precise element that makes the wine resonate. You don't change the wine, that's what's beautiful about it: the wine remains the wine. It has its personality, but you play with it, work it, help it express itself.

There are people who close the conversation, and others who make it open up and reveal itself. It's very philosophical; you go looking for something immaterial and invisible, but which is translated through something simple: the perception of power and emotion.

FA How do you work with time and tension when you taste the grape, and what you're creating? How do you imagine the outcome?

VC I always have a perspective, a projection and a prolongation. I'm always thinking of the past and the future. That's the most powerful part of what I experience. When I'm harvesting and I taste the grape of a new year, I always have this very intense resurgence of everything I'm carrying from the past. It's linked to passion and a very strong commitment for me. Commitment is about intention. I'm a seeker. When you complement that with memory, the history of what you've accumulated with the idea behind the act, you compose the act. When I'm tasting and I decide upon something, I try to put everything I am into it, all my history and the power of my intention. I like sports. I play tennis and often, it makes me think of a racket stroke: you aim for a very precise location. There's something intangible in this. You're 20 meters away, but you're aiming for one square centimeter, and you don't always get it right, but there are moments when you're spot on. That's because you carry everything with you: this knowledge, this work, this repetition, and a very strong intention. Then, you have to relax.

FA If you're tense when you're serving, it won't work.

VC In our professions, it's the same at times.

MO Tension and relaxation, it's a bit yogic.

FA There is no creation *ex nihilo*. It always comes from recollections of previous vintages.

VC It's true that creation is less instantaneous for us. There are moments of brilliance, when I come to your place, and I say to myself "wow," you've had a breakthrough! There's a ray of sunshine through the clouds. You say "that's it!" That brought me something new.

When we're tasting and I'm creating the blends, there's a moment when I taste the grape and I say: "Tomorrow, we harvest. It's there." And then, there are also moments of construction that are a bit mental and emotional, which are no longer about dazzling, but rather about decantation. There are many moments in life when clarification takes time. It's not a ray of sunshine piercing through the clouds, but rather the fog that lifts and allows the light to appear. I experience both kinds of emergence when I create.

FA Since we're talking about Dom Pérignon, a Benedictine, there's something that resonates in Cravan's cocktails, and that's equilibrium. For the Benedictines

according to Saint Benedict, it was neither too much nor too little. The perfect equilibrium between an active life and a contemplative life.

VC You went on a retreat…

FA Yes, when I was in high school, at 15 or 16 years old, I did a kind of internship known at the time as a "confrontation with working life." Instead of doing it in a bank or an insurance company, I spent a month at the Abbey of Bec-Hellouin in Normandy, with the Benedictines.

This notion of equilibrium and harmony is extremely important. We always have it in mind.

VC Yes, it's what guides us. It's linked to tension: it's an equilibrium in tension. It's very philosophical because equilibrium is a religious and cultural value that's shared by all of us, in Eastern cultures, Western cultures, etc. Harmony is quite legitimate for Dom Pérignon because it's in the roots of the founder, and what he embodies. The philosophical dimension is projected in an aesthetic. The wine and the aesthetic of the wine are at the service of something greater, which is this emotion, this plenitude, this elevation. This progression, which you experience when you go on a pilgrimage to a monastery with the hope of finding yourself.

For us, harmony is at the heart of it all; it's at the center, surrounded by five major concepts: intensity, complexity, the intensity that comes from precision. Next, there's minerality and touch. The definition of harmony in Antiquity was the capacity to take into account the complexity given to us by nature, and to organize it into something beautiful. The mono ingredient offers us an infinite diversity of nuances. And that's magnificent.

EVERYTHING IS SPIRAL

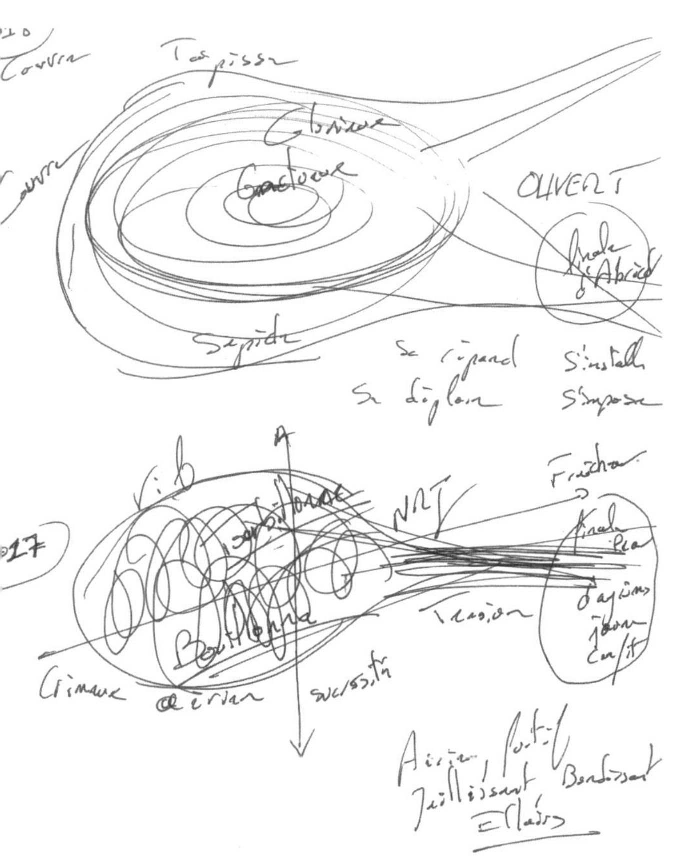

FA **To come back to a notion we touched on: the spiral echoes the fact that I always try to create cocktails with a finish that provokes a craving - more than a desire - the need to come back and taste the drink again. I'd like you to come back to this term "spiral" that you use when you create.**

VC The spiral is one of the strongest elements I inherited from my predecessor. If there's one symbolic element, it's this. Everything is spiral: we relive spring, summer, autumn, winter, growth, harvest, fermentation, all the time. We repeat the same thing, and each year it's completely different. Every year, we have a kind of progression in the repetition that helps us advance. Then, there's the form of the spiral: something that begins again, that embraces, that re-envelops. This notion of beginning again is precisely what we're seeking, because Dom Pérignon is about this loop. The embrace at a very basic, tactile level, which envelopes the palate; this sensation of somebody having just kissed you. There is an intolerable flaw when you're tasting a great wine, and that's when the finish is too short. And here, we're not talking about precision, beauty or harmony. The finish, the final sensation, is very important in wine. There's something very symbolic about it. We say: "A wine can't cheat in the finish", or "The truth about the wine is in the finish." Many wines can fool you in the attack and the initial sensations, but it's a con if there's no finish.

FA The finish is crucial for a cocktail, too.

VC It's hard to cheat when it comes to length. The finish says a lot about the wine: the flaws and disharmony appear. If you finish too dry, it's too harsh, rough and short. If nothing remains, you have nothing to say.

FA There's no length.

VC This is also something you get from relationships: sometimes we have a good time with people who make us laugh. We leave and two seconds later, we've forgotten them. And then, there are people who leave a lifelong impression on us. It's the finish that says a lot about the intention.

FA A technical question: how do you differentiate between aging and maturation?

VC Maturation is about nourishment. It's about raising something and growth - a mainstay of life, like the plant that grows as long as it's fed. When our wines are maturing, they're in our wine cellars. It's the yeast in the bottle that transforms the wine into Champagne. The yeast is this mainstay of life.

FA And they're in movement.

VC After having transformed the wine into Champagne in the bottle during the development of the "mousse", or the second alcoholic fermentation, the yeast dies and forms a solid sediment called the lees. It continues to slowly feed the wine for a very long time. It is reintegrated into the wine, reabsorbed progressively over 15, 20 years, until it disappears completely. After about 30 years, there is no longer any solid material. The wine has absorbed it all. This is a phenomenon of life, of growth. In this nourishment, there is a relationship with time and with oxygen. Oxygen is vital: it's what lets us breathe and grow, but it's also what makes us age and die. It's a fundamental, physical principle of temporality.

Either the bottle is with you at home and the wine is aging, or it is with us, maturing, and the wine is growing, taking shape. In both cases, there's a bottle sealed with a cork. And the only difference is that with us, the yeast is still there. The yeast nourishes it, and is absorbed progressively by the wine, and at the same time it reacts with the oxygen that enters, because the bottle is not hermetically sealed to gas. Oxygen enters progressively over time through the cork. This is what makes the wine oxidize progressively. At your house, since there's no barrier, this oxygen in the bottle will hit the wine directly because there's only the wine. In our cellar, there's this substrate of yeast, this material that reacts and partially protects the wine, which means that the wine undergoes a slower and more harmonious oxidation.

If we take this to a philosophical level, we observe that this is a principle that holds true throughout nature: things have the time to grow because we don't oxidize them too quickly. There's a rhythm in life. You should never do things quickly. It's the opposite of what the world invites us to do. Life, in the biological sense, invites us to go slowly. This wine, which has matured longer and aged more gently, will go further. It will be more beautiful and more complex, more true and harmonious. This isn't a declaration, it's what we've observed for 100 years. It's empirical.

FA The issue is to get it right. "With a click like a closing box," as Yeats wrote, when a poem "comes right."

VC Yes, because we tasted, we even experimented, and we kept our bottles. We kept the blends, taking out the yeast from some and keeping it in others. We noticed that it was always better, for Dom Pérignon in any case.

FA How do you envision food and wine pairing with Dom Pérignon? Beyond the liquid-liquid pairing we discussed.

VC We work on this all year round, and first of all, it's a reciprocity. We talk about an encounter, about respect. Food brings something to Dom Pérignon, and Dom Pérignon brings something to gastronomy. It's a dialogue, and more specifically, I'm looking for something that will reveal my wine, in whatever way. It might be brilliant or radical. What I'm trying to bring to gastronomy, when I'm working in dialogue with a chef, is light, energy in the alchemic sense of the term; in other words, this subtler side of elevating matter to light. That's the meaning of Champagne. Because in the end, it's got something to do with lightness, radiance in the equilibrium. So, there's a reciprocity with an intention: revelation on the one hand, light on the other.

What I saw in your work is that this creates new spaces. I hope to open up a space for the person drinking, a space of emotion. The emotion is surprise, and that will create something new. It's hard work because we can't arrive somewhere obvious, a place that's already been conquered.

FA It's the work of a tightrope-walker.

VC But you have to meet people where they are. If you shake things up too much, sometimes some people will say no. It can't work for everyone, that's not possible. It's a form of closure. We come looking for them, but they have to be looking to find something too.

FA About Cravan, I often say that what's important is curiosity. The people who come here have to be ready to accept something. If they don't accept it, I can't do anything, and that's not a problem, but you have to start from a place of curiosity.

VC Curiosity is the most basic ingredient, but we're not all curious, and I myself am not all the time. Sometimes, we're a bit closed.

CURIOSITY IS
THE MOST BASIC
INGREDIENT,

BUT WE'RE NOT
ALL CURIOUS

FA For you, food and wine pairing isn't just anecdotal. It's not an exercise, it's truly a way of opening up…

VC It's opening up and it's how your creation will experience the world. The first circle is that of gastronomy. That's how we approach it. When we prepare a new *millésime*, we know that a year ahead we're going to disgorge it. We'll get rid of the yeast in the bottle. At a certain moment, we'll say it's now, it's ready, the equilibrium is there. At that moment, we'll remove the lifeline and open the bottle to take out the yeast. We stop the movement and something happens: an equilibrium is achieved. There are several, in fact, in the life of Dom Pérignon. We stop the movement. A year before it goes on sale, because we disgorge the bottle, take out the sediment, re-cork it, and let the wine rest. That year is also the year when we will prepare the sales launch. It's like a baby, it takes its first steps with gastronomy. We watch how our wines behave with ingredients, then with recipes, dishes, and a menu. We learn a lot, because we see how it reacts in the world. It's a direct extension of the ten years in which it was conceived and developed. I bring it face to face with two things: food and people. I'll lean on the people I trust, who I know will speak to me in an informed way about how they experience the wine, because they know and love Dom Pérignon. For ten years, we've only seen it from within our team, internally…

MA Is the liquid-liquid pairing rare in reality?

VC Yes, except with sauces. It's the first time we'll do it outside of gastronomy. It's quite a powerful thing.

FA It's extremely interesting to arrive with these two liquid elements to extend, to elevate…

VC What's great is that we're exploring a new path.

FA We can compare it with a broth because we're dealing with infusions; we're more or less in the same creative direction. What interests me and fascinates me is how to develop excellence in something based on your *savoir-faire*. And above all, to never adulterate it, to keep its typical traits but move the cursor.

VC Give it this little shift to provoke something. A little bit like falling dominos. To come back to the unique aspect, the big, big difference is that this one happens in our…

FA In a glass.

VC We do it in the mouth, but we've never done it in a glass. I have no barriers. Anything is possible. I'd never say "no cocktails". We can find a balance. I'm slipping into esotericism and the invisible and immaterial side of things, but I believe a lot in sequences. There is a way to introduce things, for example in a blend. If I have ten wines and I decide on the proportions 10%, 2%, the order in which I make my blend will have an impact on the final result. There is a way for the liquid to mix, to conform in relation to the momentary tasting we will get later. In any case, you have an infusion, you put everything in at once.

FA I only have one process. Champagne first and then I tie in the rest.

VC It makes me think of dosage. What's interesting is that what we're doing together is something that's already in our inherited and handed-down *savoir-faire*. We add a *"liqueur d'expédition"* to the Champagne when we disgorge it. After removing the yeast, we add about one centiliter of an old wine that we've chosen from the dozens of wines we've made. We do tests to find the best finishing touch for the disgorged wine before re-corking it. What excites me is that there's a mirror effect with what we're doing together in our "liquid-liquid paring". It inspires me for my development and also the creation that follows.

FA Your exchange with people is always very…

VC Conceptual.

FA Yes, it goes beyond quality.

VC That's my nature. In my profession, many people are technicians. There are many country folk in the noble sense, people inspired by nature. They can be artists. They are farmers who have a respect, an understanding of nature, a capacity to express the beauty of what is given to them. We have artist winemakers and artist chefs. This category of creator, in the sense of going beyond one's perimeter, of integrating culture, is something that's quite rare in our professions, but which is developing. It's something towards which people have pushed me. I've always had it in me, but I didn't start out that way at all. I started out in my profession through the technical side.

I was lucky enough to have a mentor (Richard Geoffroy) who was a real artist. Which also helped me – because Dom Pérignon also started there – to develop something that really has artistic meaning: literature. I started working in 2005, and the first thing I did was the words of Dom Pérignon. I worked with journalists for two years to master this language.

I spend a lot of time creating collectives. I surround myself with a primary circle, a photographer, a writer, an illustrator…

FA When we met the first time, you were indeed making lots of drawings. I remember the one of the spiral very well.

VA When I drink wine, I have images that I'd like to share better. I'm in the process of reinventing the blend in relationship to our heritage. Every year, I move the lines. I have an obligation to share. I don't create alone: I have 450 winemakers, 300 cellarmen, a team of three oenologists working closely with me, and ten people who work with me on tasting all the ingredients. I need to engage in the intention.

There's a lot of dialogue in this collaboration, this exchange, and resonances at different levels on the way to do things. I see a lot of perspectives on what we do. Speaking is a need, listening is an art.

FA To come out more intelligent than you were before.

That is the advantage of clay courts (*terre battue*), the reason I love this surface more than any other (though of course mine is the perspective of a film lover, who prefers the fixed shot to the zoom): it creates fiction.

Serge Daney,
L'Amateur de tennis,
P.O.L., 2017

Tennis

CRAVAN
cocktails
U
Unexpected

V

Very Good

10
CRAVAN
plan de Paris
Sens uniques
Français, English, Deutsch, Espanol
10
10

In Paris, I always know where I am, whereas the very principle of drifting is precisely to get lost, to let yourself be carried along by moods and atmospheres… Drifting as Ralph Rumney once said, "is like visiting London with a map of Berlin."

Michèle Bernstein,
interview with Franck Perrin
CRASH Issue #99, Spring 2023.

Wandering

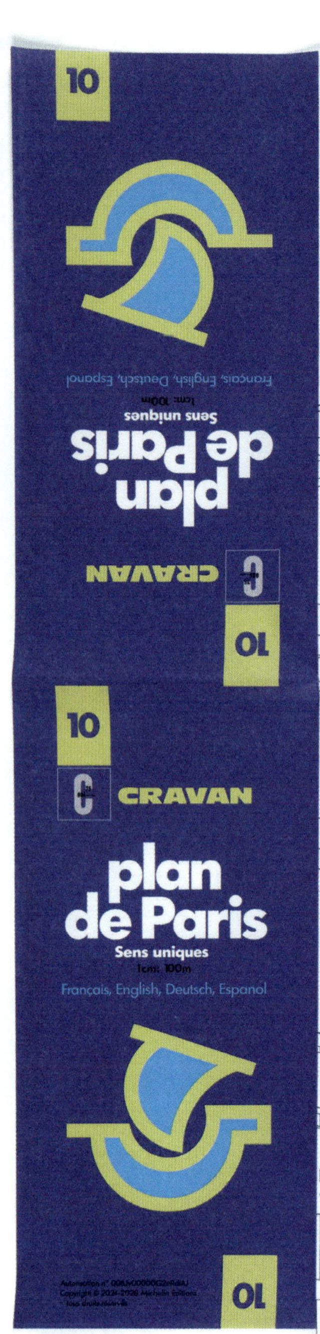
10
plan de Paris
Sens uniques
1cm: 100m
Français, English, Deutsch, Espanol
CRAVAN
10
10
CRAVAN
plan de Paris
Sens uniques
1cm: 100m
Français, English, Deutsch, Espanol
10

75
006
plan de Paris
1 / 10 000
165, Boulevard Saint-Germain, PARIS 6e

Paris
Voirie
Roads and railways
Bâtiments
Buildings
Signes divers
Miscellaneous
Verkehrswege
Vías de circulación
Gebäude
Edificios

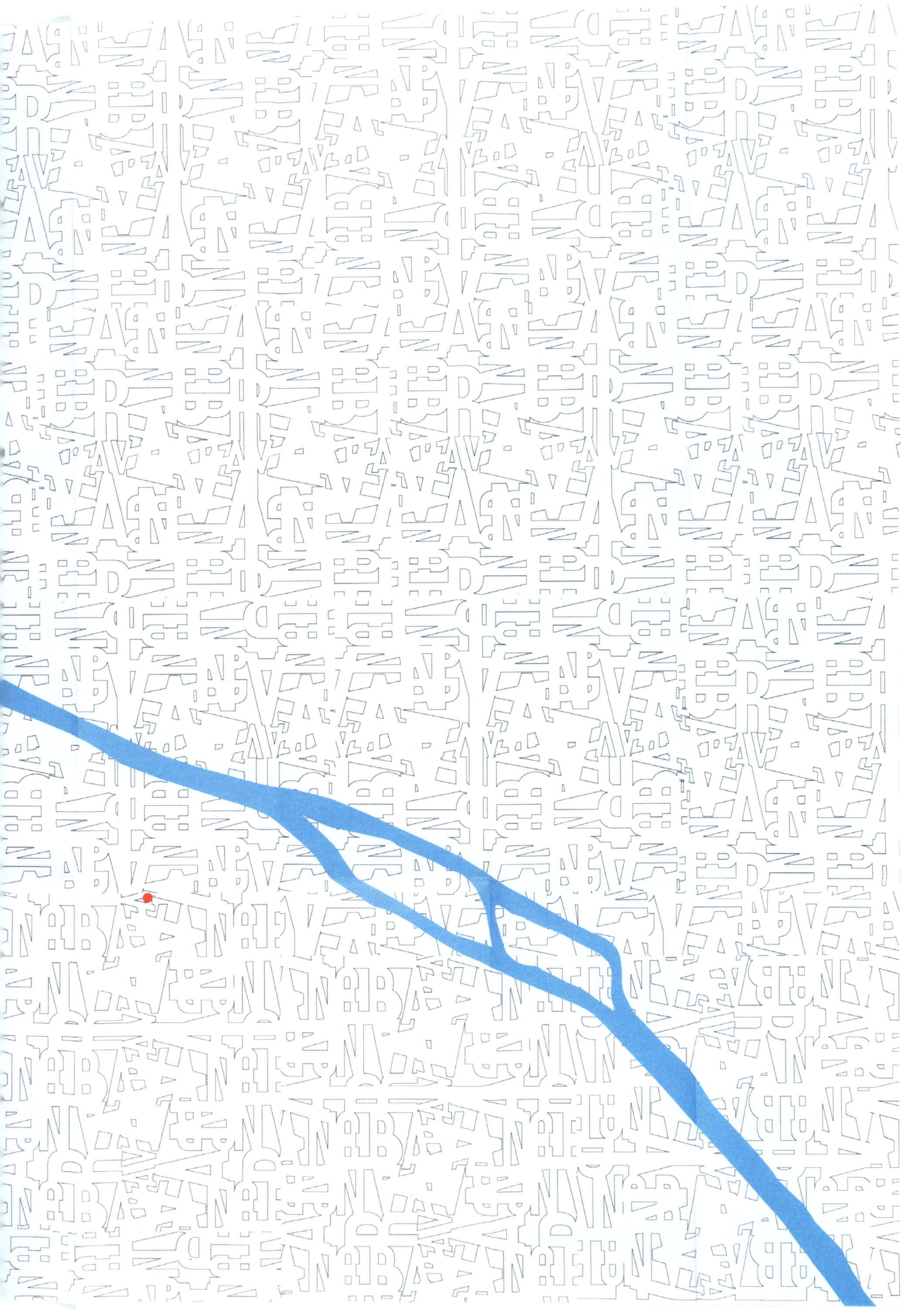

For me, the cocktail is a way of playing with time. That may be its most essential, and perhaps least recognized, dimension. A cocktail opens the door to temporal distortion. Without anchoring itself to any particular period, it allows us to take joyful liberties, even to invert the seasons: serving sunlit cocktails as a wake-up in the depths of winter, or offering bolder, more robust drinks at the height of summer.

I often choose to reserve certain preparations made with seasonal products precisely so we can serve them out of season. I particularly love putting The Lady from Shanghai on the menu long after white peach season has ended. What fascinates me is the disorienting impact of its flavor in midwinter. In a world that rightly celebrates seasonality, we prefer to bend it, sometimes even to invert it. Cocktails let us go even further with these temporal shifts. While preparing Royals, our use of infusions allowed us to taste Champagnes that immediately revealed advanced aromas, as if they had undergone years of aging. Cocktails create the illusion of maturity without the wait. They become accelerators of time, fast-forwarding today's drinks into the flavors of tomorrow.

This part of our work is exhilarating: we are developing little-known dimensions while maintaining an authentic connection to the original product. I carry this same approach into our bottled cocktails for Cravan. These are designed to be enjoyed at home, and my goal is to shift the experience of Cravan into another moment, to recreate it in all its quality and precision. I treat the cocktail as if I were setting the timer on a camera: capturing an instant and offering the chance to relive it later. I bottle the immediate, so it can be experienced again at another time. The cocktail, in short, allows me to take liberties with time.

XO

The sun dazzles me,
it rises to my head,
a sun, a light I can only call yellow:
sulfur yellow, lemon yellow,
golden yellow.

How beautiful yellow is!

Vincent van Gogh,
Letter to his brother Theo, March 1888
In Michel Pastoureau,
Yellow: The History of a Color
Éditions du Seuil, 2019

Yellow

Zest

Zest

Unless otherwise specified, all illustrations not credited below appear courtesy of Cravan. Every effort has been made to contact all the rights-holders of all the images that appear in this book. Any errors will be corrected in subsequent editions provided notification is sent to the publisher.

Principal object photography by © Elie Y. Obeid

P 1
Anonymous photographer.
Bathers at Cannes, 1930s.

P 2, 7, 12, 24–25, 30–31, 144, 238
Franck Audoux, personal images.

P 9, 214–215, 220–221
© Alice Fenwick

P 4–5
Color Harmony and Pigments,
by Hilaire Hiler, 1942.

P 15
Advertising for *Side Magazine* (An Acrobat Issue) edited by Yasmine d'O. and Sâadane Afif, 2022.

P 17
© Bernard Lipnitzki

P 26–27, 193, 198–209
© Vincent Leroux

P 45
A collage based on the cover of the first volume of the *Fantômas series*.
Fayard Editions, 1911.

P 50–51
Image extracted from the movie *Exposé du film annonce du film Scénario*. In October 2021, Jean-Luc Godard presented his idea for *Scénario*, a 6-chapter feature film combining still and moving images, halfway between reading and seeing, which was posthumously coproduced by Écran Noir in Paris in 2024.
© Ecran noir productions

P 60
Jean-Luc Godard,
Introduction to a True History of Cinema.
Albatros Editions, 1980.

P 166
Jean-Pierre Bertrand,
Etrog, 1999. Acrylic on plywood.
© Galerie Michel Rein

P 168–169
Édouard Manet,
The Lemon, 1880. Oil on canvas.

P 171
Stills extracted from *Pickpocket*,
Robert Bresson, 1959.
© Archives Robert Bresson/MK2

P 172–173
Fig. 43. "How to bandage your hands."
Fernand Cuny, *Boxing*. Nilsson Editions, first edition 1918.

P 178
Large poster of the boxing match between Jack Johnson and Arthur Cravan at the Plaza de Toros Monumental, Sunday, April 23, 1916.
Fabienne Bénédict Collection.
© Galerie 1900 ▽ 2000

P 180–183
© Galerie 1900 ▽ 2000

P 184–185
French Moderne Cocktails, Franck Audoux,
© Rizzoli New York

P 210–211
Fig. 64. "The serve."
Tennis: Hockey, Palms, Balls and Boules,
(a collective work), Pierre Lafitte & Co. Editions, 1913.

P 218
Isaac Newton,
"Colors of Thin Films,"
from *Treatise on Optics*, 1704.

P 219
Ogden Rood,
"Diagram of Contrasts,"
from *Scientific Theory of Colors*, 1879.

P 232–233
Stills from the film *Royal in Saint-Germain-des-Prés*, 2025.

P 234–235
Orson Welles, *Around the World with Orson Welles*, 1955.

P 236–237, 244
Sketches by Vincent Chaperon.

P 250 (from top to bottom):
Fig. 46. "Backhand smash during a match (Max Decugis)."
Fig. 19. "American serve (G. Ganet)."
Fig. 47. "End of backhand smash."
Tennis: Hockey, Palms, Balls and Boules, (a collective work), Pierre Lafitte & Co. Editions, 1913.

P 252–253
A collage based on *Blow-Up*,
Michelangelo Antonioni, 1966.

P 254–255
Stills from the film *Un cornet de dés*, 2025.

P 258, 260–261
Cravan: Plan de Paris, 2023

P 266
Still Life with a Porcelain Bowl, a Glass on a Gilt Stand and Lemons,
Jan Jansz van de Velde III (1620–1662).

Illustration Credits

Cocktail Index

Vincent Chaperon joined Dom Pérignon in 2005 and was appointed *chef de caves* in January 2019. His encounter with Richard Geoffroy, who served as *chef de caves* at Dom Pérignon from 1990 to 2018, marked the beginning of a thirteen-year partnership during which the two men engaged in a profound dialogue with nature, and built a relationship of trust.

Nicolas Chatenier is an author and journalist specializing in gastronomy. Author of *Mémoires de Chefs*, his latest book, *La Clé Anglaise: Géopolitique de la Gastronomie Française*, analyzes France's place on the global culinary scene.

A Belgian designer based in Paris, **Ramy Fischler** imagines spaces and objects that anticipate the uses of tomorrow. A graduate of ENSCI-Les Ateliers and former resident of the Villa Medici, he founded RF Studio in 2011, where he explores the intersections between design, interior architecture, design fiction, and technological innovation. Balancing *art de vivre* and foresight, his work ranges from hospitality to culture, from luxury to circular economy projects – including the brasserie of the National Gallery in London, and in the the Eiffel Tower, the Hilton Cannes, and the Refettorio Paris, created in collaboration with architect Nicolas Delon and artist JR.

Marie Ottavi is a journalist at *Libération*, where she writes mainly about fashion, and an author. She has written *Jacques de Bascher, Dandy de l'Ombre* (Séguier, 2017) and a biography of Karl Lagerfeld, *Karl: Une Histoire de la Mode* (Robert Laffont, 2021), recently translated into English by Rizzoli NY.

Dominique Païni is a French essayist, film critic, and exhibition curator. He served as Director of Film Productions at the Louvre from 1986 to 2000, Director of the Cinémathèque Française from 1990 to 2000, and Director of the Department of Cultural Development at the Centre Georges Pompidou from 2000 to 2005. He contributes to various publications, including *Art Press* and *Les Cahiers du Cinéma*.

Contributors

First published in the United States of America in 2026
by Rizzoli International Publications, Inc.
49 West 27th Street New York, NY 10001
www.rizzoliusa.com

The Author expresses his gratitude to all those taking part in this adventure, whether at the bar or at the office, whose presence made these connections meaningful.

A heartfelt thank-you to E.W.A. and C.B.M. for their daily support.

For Cravan
Partner-in-Charge: Caroline Grenthe

Book Design by Chloé Passavant

For Rizzoli International Publications, Inc.
Publisher: Charles Miers
Editor: Ian Luna
Project Editors: Joe Davidson & Meaghan McGovern
Production: Barbara Sadick & Eugene Lee
Proofreaders: Mary Ellen Wilson & Tricia Levi
Translation: Rebecca Cavanaugh

The Editor and Rizzoli would like to extend their appreciation to Marie Lipnitzky, Caroline Panefieu, Pete Vasconcellos and Eugene Lee for their additional support.

Printed in Italy
2026 2027 2028 2029 2030 / 10 9 8 7 6 5 4 3 2 1
ISBN: 978-0-8478-7649-5
The authorized representative in the EU for product safety and compliance is Mondadori Libri S.p.A., via Gian Battista Vico 42, Milan, Italy, 20123 www.mondadori.it

Visit us online
Instagram: @RizzoliBooks
Facebook.com/RizzoliNewYork
Youtube.com/user/RizzoliNY

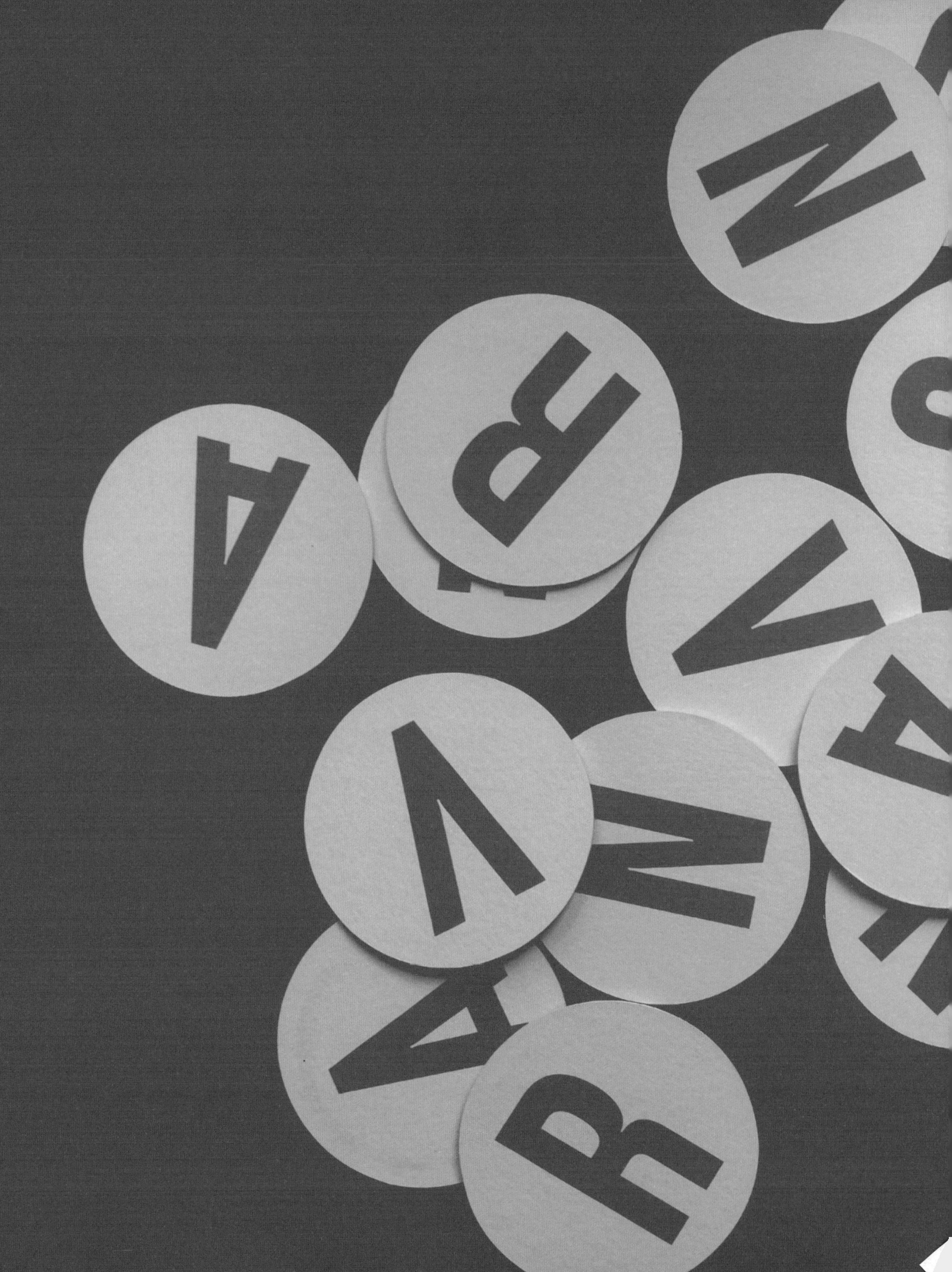